CESAR CHAVEZ

CESAR CHAVEZ

A Biography

Roger Bruns

GREENWOOD BIOGRAPHIES

GREENWOOD PRESS
WESTPORT, CONNECTICUT · LONDON

Library of Congress Cataloging-in-Publication Data

Bruns, Roger
  Cesar Chaves : a biography / Roger Bruns.
    p. cm. — (Greenwood biographies, ISSN 1540–4900)
  Includes bibliographical references and index.
  ISBN 0–313–33452–8
  1. Chavez, Cesar, 1927– 2. Labor leaders—United States—Biography.
3. Mexican Americans—Biography. 4. Agricultural laborers—Labor unions—
United States—History —20th century. I. Title. II. Series.
HD6509.C48B78 2005
331.88'13'092—dc22   2005016819

British Library Cataloguing in Publication Data is available.

Library of Congress Catalog Card Number: 2005016819
ISBN: 0–313–33452–8
ISSN: 1540–4900

First published in 2005

Greenwood Press, 88 Post Road West, Westport, CT 06881
An imprint of Greenwood Publishing Group, Inc.
www.greenwood.com

Printed in the United States of America

The paper used in this book complies with the
Permanent Paper Standard issued by the National
Information Standards Organization (Z39.48–1984).

10 9 8 7 6 5 4 3 2 1

CONTENTS

Photo essay follows page 54

SERIES FOREWORD

In response to high school and public library needs, Greenwood developed this distinguished series of full-length biographies specifically for student use. Prepared by field experts and professionals, these engaging biographies are tailored for high school students who need challenging yet accessible biographies. Ideal for secondary school assignments, the length, format and subject areas are designed to meet educators' requirements and students' interests.

Greenwood offers an extensive selection of biographies spanning all curriculum related subject areas including social studies, the sciences, literature and the arts, history and politics, as well as popular culture, covering public figures and famous personalities from all time periods and backgrounds, both historic and contemporary, who have made an impact on American and/or world culture. Greenwood biographies were chosen based on comprehensive feedback from librarians and educators. Consideration was given to both curriculum relevance and inherent interest. The result is an intriguing mix of the well known and the unexpected, the saints and sinners from long-ago history and contemporary pop culture. Readers will find a wide array of subject choices from fascinating crime figures like Al Capone to inspiring pioneers like Margaret Mead, from the greatest minds of our time like Stephen Hawking to the most amazing success stories of our day like J. K. Rowling.

While the emphasis is on fact, not glorification, the books are meant to be fun to read. Each volume provides in-depth information about the subject's life from birth through childhood, the teen years, and adulthood.

A thorough account relates family background and education, traces personal and professional influences, and explores struggles, accomplishments, and contributions. A timeline highlights the most significant life events against a historical perspective. Bibliographies supplement the reference value of each volume.

INTRODUCTION

Leaders come from all kinds of backgrounds—from the exalted pedigrees of fortune and family to the lowliest of circumstances. Some, with advantages of birth and immediate access to education and opportunity, seem from the beginning destined for greatness, their road toward success paved and straight. For others, there is the choppy path, rough and treacherous, with even survival uncertain.

Cesar Chavez was the unlikeliest of leaders.

On the Colorado River, 90 miles from its mouth in southern Arizona, is Yuma. Settled largely by Mexican immigrants, its old one-story adobe buildings with their mud roofs built to withstand the scorching desert heat, Yuma became a minor hub of commerce and agriculture. It was here in 1927 that Chavez, son of a Mexican American small-scale farmer and his wife, began his own journey.

His story is not atypical, at least that of his early years—a Depression-wracked family that loses its home and is forced into scratching out a living by working as migrant field workers in California; a close-knit family sharing strong personal and religious bonds; an Hispanic American boy facing "No Mexicans Allowed" discrimination and taunts by his teachers whenever he began to speak Spanish; a teenage boy looking for a way out who joins the U.S. Navy only to find similar cultural hatred; a young man who returns to his family, marries, and has children. His life as he became a man was not unusual.

But this man had fire. He hated the injustices meted out to his family and other migrant workers. They were on American labor's last rung, thousands of individuals making a pittance for their work, living in desperate and inhumane conditions, with barely a present and not much of a future, and with few rights or leaders on which to lean.

They found a champion in Cesar Chavez. When he began to work for a social service agency in California, he started to see possibilities of making a difference for those in need. When he befriended a priest who inspired him to read serious literature, such as the writings of Mohandas Gandhi, new worlds of learning opened. When he watched Martin Luther King Jr. and other civil rights leaders organize marches, demonstrations, and other nonviolent protests, he saw examples of how the poorest and least powerful could force social change.

His dream was to found a labor union of farmworkers. He had no money, no political connections, and no experience. He was not a particularly dynamic personality and had no special talent as a public speaker. The dream, he knew, was almost fanciful. Nevertheless, through determination, grit, and a dogged will to win, he forged a movement that successfully challenged powerful entrenched economic and political interests and helped thousands of Mexican Americans to new cultural self-awareness.

He did found a union, the United Farm Workers of America; he helped improve working conditions, and he influenced political figures of national standing. By the time his work was done, his picture hung in the homes of many people who had never met him. Streets in a number of cities took on his name.

In the early years of the movement, some suggested that none of this was possible. Chavez's response: "*Sí, se puede!*" (It can be done). This is his story.

TIMELINE OF EVENTS IN
THE LIFE OF CESAR CHAVEZ

March 31, 1927	Cesar Estrada Chavez is born, the son of Librado Chavez and Juana Estrada Chavez in Yuma, Arizona, on the small farm that his grandfather homesteaded in the 1880s.
1937	After Cesar's father, Librado, is forced from his farm, the Chavez family becomes migrant workers in California.
1942	After his father is hurt in a car accident and cannot work, quits school to work in the fields with his brother and sister.
1944	Is arrested in a segregated Delano, California, movie theater for sitting in the "whites only" section and held in custody for one hour. Joins the U.S. Navy
1946	Is discharged from the navy and returns to his family in Delano; resumes work in the fields.
1948	Marries Helen Fabela. The two have eight children: Fernando (1949), Silvia (1950), Linda (1951), Eloise (1952), Anna (1953), Paul (1957), Elizabeth (1958), and Anthony (1958).
1952	Moves to San Jose and works in a lumber mill. Meets Father Donald McDonnell, a Catholic priest from San Francisco sent to work with the farm laborers. Reads the papal encyclicals on

labor, books on labor history, the teachings of St. Francis of Assisi, and Louis Fisher's *The Life of Gandhi*.

Is recruited by Fred Ross to be an organizer for Community Service Organization (CSO).

1958–1959   Is sent to Oxnard, California, by the CSO to confront the bracero program, a system used by the growers to depress wages and exploit the farm laborers. Organizes a boycott of local merchants, sit-down strikes in the fields to challenge the hiring of braceros, and protest against the lack of jobs for local residents.

1962   Resigns from the CSO and moves with his wife and eight small children to Delano, California, to start the National Farm Workers Association (NFWA).

September 30, 1962 First meeting of NFWA convenes in Fresno, California. Chavez is elected president.

1964   NFWA has 1,000 dues-paying members and fifty locals. Launches the newspaper *El Malcriado* as the official voice of NFWA.

September 16, 1965 On Mexican Independence Day, NFWA votes to join a strike against Delano-area grape growers already begun that month by the mostly Filipino American members of the Agricultural Workers Organizing Committee (AWOC).

NBC screens "A Harvest of Shame," a television special that depicts the tragic conditions of migrant laborers in the United States.

NFWA, along with AWOC, launches a boycott against the Schenley Vineyards Corporation, DiGiorgio Fruit Corporation, S&W Fine Foods, and TreeSweet.

March 17, 1966   Leads strikers on a 340-mile march from Delano to the steps of the state capitol in Sacramento. Rally in Sacramento on April 10 draws 10,000 people.

During the march and after a four-month boycott, Schenley Vineyards negotiates an agreement with NFWA, the first genuine union contract between a grower and farm workers' union in U.S. history.

AWOC and the NFWA merge to form a united union within the AFL-CIO. The United Farm

Workers Organizing Committee (UFWOC; later to become the United Farm Workers of America, AFL-CIO) is formed under the direction of Chavez.

1967   UFWOC strikes the Giumarra Vineyards Corporation, California's largest table grape grower. In response to a UFWOC boycott, other grape growers allow Giumarra to use their labels. The UFWOC then begins a boycott of all California table grapes.

DiGiorgio Fruit Corporation, a major grape grower, signs labor negotiation contract with UFWOC.

Union moves from its cramped offices to a new complex of buildings called "The Forty Acres."

February 14, 1968   Begins a fast to encourage a stop to violence among picketers in the Giumarra strike. Fasts for twenty-five days to rededicate his movement to nonviolence. Senator Robert F. Kennedy attends mass where Chavez breaks fast. Civil Rights leader Dr. Martin Luther King Jr. sends a telegram of support.

March 24, 1968   Announces in Los Angeles plans for a "worldwide boycott" of California grapes.

1969   UFW turns its attention to pesticide problems facing workers in the field.

May 10, 1969   International Grape Boycott Day is declared.

Organizes a march through the Coachella and Imperial Valleys to the U.S.-Mexico border to protest grower use of undocumented immigrants from Mexico as strike-breakers.

May 29, 1970   First table grape contract is signed with more than twenty California growers.

Spring-summer 1970   To keep the UFWOC out of California lettuce and vegetable fields, most Salinas Valley growers sign contracts with the Teamsters Union. Some 10,000 Central Coast farm workers respond by walking out on strike. Chavez calls for a nation-wide boycott of lettuce.

National Chicano Moratorium Rally held in East Los Angeles to protest the Vietnam War. Chavez sends a strong letter of support to the organizers.

December 10, 1970   Is jailed in Salinas for refusing to obey a court order to stop the boycott against Bud Antle Company lettuce. Coretta Scott King, widow of Dr. Martin Luther King Jr., and Ethel Kennedy, widow of Robert F. Kennedy, visit Chavez in jail.

1971–1972   With its membership growing to around 80,000, Chavez union is chartered as an independent affiliate by the AFLCIO; it becomes the United Farm Workers of America, AFL-CIO (UFW).

Spring-summer 1973   When the UFW's three-year table grape contracts come up for renewal, owners instead sign contracts with the Teamsters, sparking a bitter three-month strike by grape workers. Thousands of strikers are arrested for violating anti-picketing injunctions, hundreds are beaten, dozens are shot, and two are murdered. Responding to the violence, Chavez calls off the strike and begins a second grape boycott.

September 21, 1973   UFW holds its first constitutional convention in Fresno, where 346 delegates representing 60,000 farm workers adopt a constitution.

1975   California Labor Relations Act is enacted. It is the first law governing farm labor organizing in the continental United States. It provides for secret ballot elections, the right to boycott, voting rights for migrant seasonal workers, and control over the timing of elections.

                      Chavez leads a 1,000-mile march through the Imperial and San Joaquin Valleys to advertise upcoming union elections.

                      After years of lobbying by the UFW, a Supreme Court ruling (*Sebastian Carmona et al. vs. Division of Industrial Safety, 1975*) and a California administrative ruling outlaw the use of *el cortito*, the short-handled hoe.

July 31, 1979   Leads members of the UFW on a twelve-day march from San Francisco to Salinas to dramatize the union's six-month strike against the state's lettuce growers. Calls for a boycott against Chiquita brand bananas, A&W root beer, and Morrell Meats, all subsidiaries of United Brands, which controls Sun Harvest.

September 1979	After a strike and boycott, the UFW wins its demands for a significant pay raise and other contract improvements from Sun Harvest.
1983–1990	Republican California Governor George Deukmejian closes down enforcement of the state's historic farm labor law. Thousands of farm workers lose their UFW contracts. Many are fired and blacklisted.
1984	Announces that the UFW is embarking on a new grape boycott. To reach more people, Chavez emphasizes the issue of pesticide residues on fruit.
1987	UFW produces *The Wrath of Grapes*, a movie in which graphic footage shows birth defects and high rates of cancer produced by pesticide poisoning among farm workers and consumers.
August 1988	At age 61, Chavez conducts his last public fast for thirty-six days in Delano to call attention to farm workers and their children stricken by pesticides.
Spring 1992	Leads vineyard walkouts in the Coachella and San Joaquin Valleys and wins first industry-wide pay hike for workers in eight years. In the Salinas Valley, leads more than 10,000 workers in a protest march for better conditions in the field.
April 23, 1993	After fasting for a few days to gain moral strength, dies in his sleep.
April 29, 1993	At his funeral more than 35,000 people follow the casket for three miles, from Delano to Keene, California.
August 1994	President Bill Clinton posthumously presents to Chavez the Medal of Freedom, America's highest civilian honor. His widow, Helen, receives the medal during a White House ceremony.

Chapter 1

IN THE FIELDS

Stooped over in the intense sun along the rows of crops, the migrants worked from early morning till nearly dark. In the lettuce fields and the pea fields, in the grape orchards and cherry groves, they harvested—men and women alongside young boys and girls, day after day, their bodies contorted in painful routine.

At night, they returned to the housing camps—dirty, cramped, run-down shacks, converted chicken coops, and storage sheds, none with running water or electricity, almost all of them infested with mosquitoes. Dozens of families shared a single outhouse. Water came from nearby irrigation ditches. They never had enough food. Children went to school only when they were not needed in the fields. Their families wandered from one job to another, so many of the youngsters attended several schools a year, some of them for only a few weeks.

Americans driving the roads of California, Arizona, or other western states could glimpse from the highways groups of pickers in the fields. Stoop labor must be dreadful, many drivers undoubtedly remarked to their traveling companions. But the distance from the roads to the pickers was as close as nearly anyone would ever come to the lives of the migrants. Few imagined their plight.

In 1965 grape pickers in California made an average of less than a dollar an hour. Many workers suffered injury or death from disease or accident. The average life expectancy of a farm worker was forty-nine years.

One boy of Mexican descent who grew up with a migrant worker family in California remembered the constant traveling. Most winters they spent around Brawley, California, where they worked the fields harvesting carrots, peas, and mustard greens. In the broccoli fields, he remembered, the workers waded in water and mud that rose to the level of the youngsters' necks. Their hands, he said, were often numb with cold. "In late May," he said," we had two or three options: Oxnard for beans, Beaumont for cherries, or the Hemet area for apricots. I think we did all at one time or another. From there we worked in corn and chili peppers, and picked fresh lima beans for fifty cents a basket. Then in August through part of October, we had grapes, prunes and tomatoes. We would go before those crops started and wait in a camp until they were ready. Then we did cotton from October through Christmas. It was hard work, but there was nothing else."[1]

The boy's name was Cesar Chavez. Unlike anyone before him, he would make a difference for migrant workers.

Chavez was born near Yuma, Arizona, on March 31, 1927, the second of 6 children of Librado and Juana Chavez. His fraternal grandfather, Cesario "Papa Chayo," had crossed the border into Arizona from Mexico in 1888, settling on a farm in the North Gila Valley desert, along the Colorado River. Born an indentured servant in Chihuahua, Mexico, Cesario fled the hacienda after an argument with the landowner's son. After crossing the border, he found work as a mule-skinner, near some Southern Arizona mines. He was illiterate. His wife, Dorotea, "Mama Tella," could read both Spanish and Latin, a skill she learned as an orphan in a Mexican convent.

Cesario and Dorotea had 15 children, who helped build his farm. One of his sons, Librado, who was two years old when he came to the United States with the family, stayed with his parents on the farm. In 1924, he married Juana Estrada, whose family had also migrated north from Chihuahua.

The family worked the land, cared for horses and cows, and opened a small grocery store. Living in their small adobe house, the family, although not wealthy, lived comfortably. Aunts and uncles surrounded young Chavez in the community. He was particularly close to his brother Richard, two years younger than himself, and his cousin, Manuel Chavez. He had an older sister, Rita, born in 1925, and two younger sisters, Helena (who died very young) and Vicky (1933). His youngest brother, Lenny, was born in 1934.

For a time, Librado operated a small automobile repair shop and, later, a poolroom. He also supplemented his income by driving stagecoaches and twenty-mule teams. Local residents also elected him to be a postmaster.

Chavez always remembered a loving family that surrounded him, centered in a Roman Catholic faith that played a central role throughout his life. Grandmother Mama Tella told stories about the importance of setting a moral example in the community, of taking responsibility not only for one's own actions but also in aggressively seeking to help others, regardless of their background.

Guided by Mama Tella, the Chavez children learned the rituals and trappings of the Catholic church. All his life, Chavez would look to those teachings and his own religious impulses for guidance. He would come to believe, as Mama Tella had taught, that faith imparted strength and direction and that religion could bring unity and power not only to individual lives but to groups of people as they struggled for just causes. Later reflecting on the wisdom of his grandmother, Chavez attributed much of his understanding of human nature and the human condition to those early teachings.

Although his mother could neither read nor write, she taught through stories and proverbs lessons about honesty and nonviolence, about sacrifice and obedience, that Chavez would absorb as his own moral compass. Devoutly religious, she set an example to Chavez with her kindness and generosity to those in need. On many occasions, drifters and hobos who moved past their Gila Valley home were invited to the dinner table.

His father taught him that it was honorable to fight for the rights of others and to value labor and personal responsibility. When migrant workers began to organize unions to fight for better working conditions in the fields, Librado was always an enthusiastic leader. Chavez said of the examples set by his family: "It came naturally to us to hope for the future and to want to make things better in the world. It seemed so obvious that God wanted more equality and more justice, and that God expected people to work for these things."[2]

From his family, Chavez heard stories about the treatment of poor workers in both Mexico and the United States. He heard about hacienda landowners in Mexico paying a pittance for hard labor in the fields. He heard about the easy life of the owners and grand mansions they erected on the outskirts of Mexican towns, in stark contrast to the poverty of 99 percent of the people around them. He heard about the rich farm owners in the United States, exploiting the labor of poor workers fleeing poverty in Mexico to find a better life north of the border. He learned how cheaply the farm owners valued the lives and the work of laborers, even though that labor made their profits and rich lifestyles possible.

At an early age, Cesar began to believe in the moral goodness of those who worked the land. He saw the generosity of his own family first hand and how, despite their own poverty, they had tried to help out those who were desperately in need. When the Chavez family read the bible, they took to heart those passages that lauded the working classes and scolded the money-lenders. To Cesar, the poor classes were those who were living a moral and Christian life. "I had more happy moments as a child than unhappy moments," Chavez later said.[3]

ON THE ROAD

During the upheaval of the Great Depression and the resulting massive unemployment and economic losses sustained across the country, the Chavez family, as many others, faced the troubled times with little or no financial resources upon which to fall back. Unable to pay property taxes on their beloved farm, they were forced off the land. It was 1937 and Chavez was ten years old. The relative stability he and the others had experienced on the farm was about to be shattered.

Before the family left the farm, Chavez later remembered, the new owners bulldozed the land that the family had worked so hard. The machine itself became a symbol to Chavez of the power that society's wealthy could wield against those with nothing. "It was a monstrous thing," he wrote, "Its motor blotted out the sound of crickets and bull-frogs and the buzzing of the flies. As the tractor moved along, it tore up the soil, leveling it, and destroyed the trees, pushing them over like they were nothing. . . . And each tree, of course, means quite a bit to you when you're young. They are a part of you. We grew up there, saw them every day, and they were alive, they were friends. When we saw the bulldozer just uprooting those trees, it was tearing at us too."[4]

Librado and Juana, with their three sons and two daughters, loaded in their car the few possessions they could take with them from Arizona and joined the thousands of other Depression-era families on the road to California and its vast harvest lands where the dispossessed and poverty-wracked might find temporary work.

Chavez would attend more than 50 different schools by the time he finished the eighth grade. Years afterward, he talked about the irony of his later career and what might have been if the family had been able to hold on to the farm. "If we had stayed there," he said, "possibly I would have been a grower. God writes in exceedingly crooked lines."[5]

For the Chavez family, as for so many others who migrated to California in search of fruit and vegetable picking jobs, survival was hour by hour and day by day—finding work, riding to the fields at three o'clock in the morning, the long, sun-drenched days in the rows of crops fending off the constant fatigue and pain, the brief respites at night, and the beginning of the same cycle over and over again. The family moved from harvest to

harvest in towns such as Brawley and Oxnard, and in such lush agricultural areas Salinas Valley, known as the "The Salad Bowl of the World"
for its production of lettuce, broccoli, mushrooms, and other crops.

The Chavez family joined more than 200,000 migrant farmworkers
who had traveled to California in search of work. They were refugees from
the Depression—poor whites from the South and Southwest uprooted not
only by economic deprivation but by drought; black sharecroppers from
the South who had lost their land; Mexicans recently arrived from south
of the border; and Mexican Americans, such as the Chavez family, also in
search of any kind of jobs that could support them and their families.

The Chavez family were now in a growing workforce critically important to American agriculture during the harvest seasons and yet jarring
to the American social fabric—thousands of men, women, and children
willing to work for meager wages and yet largely unaccounted for in the
organized systems of American culture, from its schools and courts to its
social programs and constitutional freedoms.

From the Imperial Valley in the south to San Jose in the north, the
Chavez family traveled from one harvesting job to another. Inevitably
they, along with other migrant workers, found low wages, pitiful working
conditions, and, on occasion, unscrupulous labor contractors.

It was during their first year on the road that the family signed up with
a labor contractor near Fresno, California, to pick grapes in a vineyard.
After working for the first week, Librado asked for the weekly pay. The
contractor explained that no payments would be made until the entire job
was completed. The family continued working until the entire vineyard
was picked clean. When, on the last day of the job, the family searched
for the contractor and their paycheck, he was gone.

Faced with such indignities and humiliations, the family managed to
earn only about $300 in their first year of work. Ardently trying to make it
work for them, they continued moving from valley to valley, from harvest
to harvest, trying to keep afloat. Cesar's sister Rita later recalled, "We had
never worked for anybody else. We never lived away from our home. Here
we come to California, and we were lucky we got a tent. Most of the time
we were living under a tree, with just a canvas on top of us."[6]

Increasingly, the work left them physically debilitated and relatively
powerless to do anything to end their stifling transience. Nevertheless,
they kept going, striving to keep their spirits high and to look forward to
better days.

For a young boy, the life was a thief of some of the simple pleasures
of teenagers. When the boys found a chance they played stickball with
friends. Richard and Cesar remained close their entire lives.

In time, all of the family members began to harbor an increasing militancy that Chavez later saw as instinctive. In late November 1938, the frantic moving from location to location temporarily ended on the coast of Southern California, near Oxnard. It stopped because their car stopped and the family had no money to repair it. They were stranded.

They began the winter in a makeshift tent. Using a 50-gallon can for a stove, they burned wood scraps for heat. Richard, later remembered, "There was this nice lady there, and she had a vacant lot that she let us use. So we put up this tent. It was a very small tent—I guess about 8 by 10. That's all we had. All the family stayed there. And it rained that winter. Oh, it rained. Rain, rain, rain. We had to go to school barefoot. We had no shoes. I can't forget it."[7]

While Librado and Juana managed to find a few picking jobs, the children did odd jobs around town. Together, they earned enough money for food. Gradually, they were able to fix the car and make their way back south to the Imperial Valley.

For the next couple of years Brawley, California, became a home base. As they traveled northward each early spring from job to job, they gained greater knowledge about the rotation of crops and the successive harvests; they gained a better insight into the location of the more reliable jobs; and they became better aware of the pitfalls to avoid. They learned what to expect from the weather, where to camp when no housing was available, how to find the areas that provided shelter from the winter fog and rain and the heat of summer. They picked peas, lettuce, tomatoes, figs, prunes, grapes, and apricots. In late November the cycle ended, and they headed south again, hoping that the old car would again make it back to Brawley.

LESSONS OF INTOLERANCE

As it was for most Mexican American children first thrust into the local school systems in the southwestern United States, Chavez and his family suffered in numerous ways. For children such as Chavez who grew up speaking only Spanish at home, the sudden demands of learning in an English-only classroom setting were daunting. The teachers and school administrators were overwhelmingly Anglo and many did not hide their contempt toward Hispanic culture and language. When Chavez tried to answer questions in Spanish, teachers would whip a trusty ruler across his knuckles. Cesar later remembered one teacher who forced Hispanic students to run laps around the track when they tried to speak Spanish in class.

Also, simple human relationships between culturally diverse children in school were both challenging and frustrating. The phrase "dirty Mexican," Chavez remembered later, often rolled easily off the tongues of fellow classmates. Fights between whites and Mexican American students usually favored the whites because of their numbers and also because of the tendency of teachers to decide disputes in favor of the Anglo students. Before he was ten years old, Chavez had learned hard lessons of prejudice and injustice.

Those lessons would multiply. In Brawley, the residents were segregated and Mexican Americans were told at an early age not to go into the Anglo section of town. One summer, Richard and Cesar set up a shoeshine stand on a street near the Anglo section to make extra money. One of the diners near their stand was noted for its excellent hamburgers and the boys, after one especially good day of shines, decided to try them out. They were turned away. They had ignored the signs that clearly said "Whites Only." Even though they were second-generation Americans, to the proprietors of the diner they were still Mexicans and therefore second-class citizens.

More than once the family members were turned away from establishments by dispiriting signs announcing "We Don't Sell to Mexicans." Chavez later remembered the humiliation of seeing other signs on stores that read "No Dogs or Mexicans Allowed." Many movie theaters were off limits. Some aggressive white children once forced him to wear a sign that said "I am a clown. I speak Spanish." One California fruit grower expressed an attitude toward Hispanic laborers common to other fellow growers. A picker of Mexican background, he said, had slavelike docility. "He is a fellow easy to handle and very quiet in his living, a man who lends himself very well to ranch labor, a man who gives us no trouble at all. He takes his orders and follows them."[8] From his earliest childhood days, Chavez, as did other Hispanic children in the United States, learned limitations rather than possibilities.

In June 1939 the 12-year old Chavez saw his father join an infant union in the dried fruit industry. Although a strike organized by the workers was quickly broken, Librado walked a picket line and took part in meetings in some of the homes of workers. Chavez was wide-eyed at the brief but bustling activity and admired the determination of the men to improve their conditions. Even at such a young age, in seeing these early, halting attempts at organizing workers, Chavez felt a stirring motivation to become an active union leader himself and to be part of a movement that would bring justice and a better life to other field workers.

FIGHTING BACK

In 1942, when Chavez was 15 years old, his father was seriously injured in an automobile accident. The boy dropped any ideas he or the family had regarding his attending high school. It was now important for the family's survival that he should become the primary money earner. For a time, with his brother and sister, he thinned lettuce and beets with a short-handled hoe (el cortito), a tool notoriously hard to use for any lengthy period of time because of the backbreaking posture into which the users were forced to work.

Chavez later remembered the work in the lettuce fields:

I would chop out a space with a short-handled hoe in the right hand while I felt with my left to pull out all but one plant. I made the next chop. There was a rhythm, it went very fast. It had to, it was all piece rate, so much by acre, so much a row. It was really inhuman. Every time I see lettuce, that's the first thing I think of, some human being had to thin it And it's just like being nailed to a cross You have to walk twisted, as you're stooped over, facing the row, and walking perpendicular to it You are always trying to find the best position because you can't walk completely sideways, it's too difficult, and if you turn the other way, you can't thin.[9]

At a time when most teenagers were beginning high school, Chavez was now dealing with the injustices that were part of the migrant worker's experience and beginning to see in a more firsthand, personal way the suffering and cultural prejudices under which they labored. He saw companies charging exorbitant rents on the workers' quarters, money that was taken directing out of their paychecks.

Isolated in the fields, the workers had no choice but to stay in those shacks and no choice but to buy food and other supplies from makeshift stores owned by the companies that also charged outrageous prices. He saw unscrupulous labor contractors hired by the companies skim off a portion of their salaries for the opportunity to work. He saw contractors make payroll deductions for Social Security and then pocket the money.

These practices were not unusual in such hardscrabble labor conditions in which work was scarce and those seeking it plentiful in numbers. Nevertheless, for the Hispanic workers facing the added cultural circumstances, the conditions were particularly daunting.

In 1943, the Chavez family settled in Delano, California, in the center of the crop-rich San Joaquin Valley. The family's migrations throughout the farmlands of California had often led to Delano. It was in Delano that the young teenager began to display, as did many other Mexican American youngsters, the *pachuco* or zoot suit look. The style was from Los Angeles, and it spoke of the rebelliousness, sense of anger, and frustration of Mexican American youth. The look was sleek—a long suit coat with tapered pants, a low-hanging watch chain, and a wide-brimmed hat covering long ducktail haircuts. To the Mexican American youngsters who formed gangs of *pachucos*, this was a cultural statement, a symbol of resistance against the demands of assimilation into the white culture. It was cool and slightly dangerous-looking. To the general public it could also seem frightening, if not un-American. Chavez eagerly adopted the look, began to smoke cigarettes, and generally enjoyed striking a bit of anxiety among others in the community.

One day in 1943, Chavez walked into a malt shop in Delano and met Helen Fabela, a pretty, dark-haired girl about his own age, who worked as a clerk in a grocery store patronized by the migrant workers. Fifteen years old and shy, she had already experienced, since she was seven, many of the tough weeks and months in the grape and berry fields of California. She had lost her father a few years earlier, and the family, like most of the migrants, was under severe financial burden. As had Chavez, Helen would soon drop out of high school to help the family pay bills. The two began to ride around Delano in his clunky, gas-guzzling car and occasionally to attend the movies. It was the beginning of a lifelong bond.

In 1944, at age 17, Chavez left his life in the fields and joined the navy. "I was doing sugar-beet thinning, the worst backbreaking job," he said, "and I remember telling my father, Dad, I've had it. Neither my mother or father wanted me to go, but I joined up anyway."[10] Chavez was sent to the Mariana Islands and then to Guam. He served two years as a deckhand and painter on a destroyer escort.

He remembered the experience as two of the worst years of his life, not only because of the war experience itself, with its death and destruction, but also because of the discrimination within the military against nonwhites. When he joined the military, Chavez had some hope that he might acquire a trade or skill that would advance him in the larger society. What he found was a system not unlike the one he left behind—one that kept blacks and Hispanics at the lower end of the system, with the least desirable jobs.

While on 72-hour leave from the navy, Chavez returned briefly to Delano. He attended a theater with Helen that specifically sectioned off a quarter of the seats for "colored only." "Colored" included African Americans, Filipinos, and Mexican Americans. Chavez ignored the sign.

Later, he said, "I thought an awful lot about it, but I hadn't planned anything.... It wasn't a question of sitting there because it was more comfortable or anything ... I wanted a free choice. Or at least this is how I rationalize it now. I think it was a coincidence that I decided to challenge it. But I was very frightened."[11]

When Chavez refused to leave his seat, the theater owners took action. "The assistant manager came. The girl who sold the popcorn came. Then the manager came. They tried to pull me up, and I said, 'No, you have to break my arms before I get up.'"[12]

Finally, the local police extricated the young man from his seat and took him to the police station, where he received a long lecture from the chief of police. After spending a short time in custody, he was released and not charged with a specific crime. That night in Delano was his first brazen act of civil disobedience. There would be many others.

Following his stint in the Navy, Chavez returned to the United States in 1946. He saw no alternative but to return to work in the fields of California.

Chavez recalled that

> When I was 19, I was picking cotton in Corcoran. A car with loud speakers came around. The speakers were saying: "Stop Working. You're not making a living. Come downtown to a rally instead." My brother and I left, with many others. 7000 cotton pickers gathered in a little park in the center of Corcoran. There was a platform and a union leader got up and started talking to all the workers about "the cause." I would have died right then if someone had told me how and why to die for our cause. But no one did. There was a crisis, and a mob, but there was no organization, and nothing came of it all. A week later everyone was back picking cotton in the same field at the same low wages. It was dramatic. People came together. Then it was over. That won't organize farm workers.[13]

The members of the Chavez family, including Cesar, did join the National Farm Labor Union, a branch union affiliated with the American Federation of Labor. Organized by Ernesto Galarza, a Mexican American sociologist, author, and labor organizer, the infant union organized a number of strikes across California in the1940s, most notably against Di Giorgio Corporation, one of the largest fruit growers in the United States. Although his strikes netted few gains for the workers who joined him, Galarza's pioneering efforts drew admiring notice from Chavez.

When Chavez himself would set out on his own organizing campaigns, Galarza would be there as an advisor.

This refusal to suffer indignity and injustice without a fight burned hotly in the young Chavez. His family had fought; he would fight on. "I don't want to suggest that we were radical," he said later, "but I know we were probably one of the strikingest families in California, the first ones to leave the fields if anybody shouted 'Huelga!' [strike!]."[14]

Huelga would become a central part of Cesar Chavez's life.

NOTES

1. Kim Benita Furumoto, "Viva La Causa! Cesar Chavez Remembered," *Diatribe*, May 1993, http://www.sfsu.edu/~cecipp/cesar_chavez/remembered.htm.

2. Rebecca Valbuena, "Young Cesar E. Chavez: The Early Years of an American Hero," *Appleseeds*, February 2002, 2.

3. California Curriculum Project Hispanic Biographies, http://www.sfsu.edu/~cecipp/cesar_chavez/chavezhome.htm.

4. Cletus E. Daniel, "Cesar Chavez and the Unionization of California Farm Workers," in *Labor Leaders in America*, edited by Melvyn Dubofsky and Warren Van Tine (Urbana: University of Illinois Press, 1987), 350–365.

5. Ibid.

6. Susan Ferriss and Ricardo Sandoval, *The Fight in the Fields: Cesar Chavez and the Farmworkers Movement* (Orlando, FL: Paradigm Productions, Inc., 1997), 10.

7. "The Little Strike That Grew to *La Causa*," *Time* (4 July 1969), 20.

8. Richard Del Castillo and Richard Garcia, *Cesar Chavez: A Triumph of Spirit* (Norman: University of Oklahoma Press, 1995), 9.

9. Jacques Levy, *Cesar Chavez: Autobiography of La Causa*, http://chavez.cde.ca.gov/ModelCurriculum/Teachers/Lessons/Resources/Documents/Chavez_Biography_by_Levy.PDF.

10. Ferriss and Sandoval, 33.

11. Ibid.

12. "The Little Strike That Grew," 20.

13. "Viva la Causa: Cesar E. Chavez, Interviewed by Wendy Goepel," originally published in *Farm Labor* 1, no. 5 (April 1964), available at http://www.sfsu.edu/~cecipp/cesar_chavez/lacausa.htm.

14. Furumoto.

Chapter 2

NONVIOLENT PROTEST AND VISIONS OF BETTERMENT

On October 22, 1948, Cesar Chavez married Helen Fabela. They honeymooned on the coast of California and visited historic Spanish missions from Sonoma to San Diego. When they returned to Delano, they continued working in the fields.

Thin, five-foot six inches tall, with jet-black hair, Chavez was 21 years old at the time of his wedding. It had been a hard youth. His body was muscled but already suffering a toll from the years in the fields. Throughout his life, he would experience extensive back pain, a condition familiar to most migrant field laborers. Outwardly shy and unimposing, Chavez harbored strong passions to fight back at the people and the conditions that had made his own life and that of his family, friends, and fellow workers so grinding.

The daughter of farm workers, Helen shared deeply the social concerns that had begun to influence her husband strongly and shape the directions in which he saw their lives moving. Together, they began, in whatever spare time they had available, to learn the requirements necessary for citizenship and to teach migrant farm workers to read and write so they could pass the required test.

In 1949, Helen gave birth to Fernando, their first of eight children. Sylvia, their second child, arrived a year later. In order to support the growing family, Chavez took a series of jobs in the fields. Soon, however, he managed to land a full-time job in a lumberyard in Crescent City, in Northern California close to the Oregon border. Along with his brother Richard and his cousin Manuel Chavez, Cesar and Helen packed their belongings and took their families to the damp pine woods, where

Richard had built a shack for them. Although the constant drizzling weather and the muddy conditions in the woods began to weigh on all of them, the job was a breakthrough for Chavez, an experience that he was able to use to get a job in another lumber mill back in familiar territory in San Jose.

In 1952, along with Richard and the others, Chavez left Crescent City and moved into an area in southeast San Jose called Sal Si Puedes. In California's agricultural areas, new Mexican American barrios grew as seasonal migratory laborers such as the Chavez family became settled. Sal Si Puedes ("Get out if you can") was one of those barrios.

Seemingly lost in a work cycle that would lead to nowhere but poverty, sickness, and defeat, Chavez fought off discouragement. Later, he said, "We thought the only way we could get out of the circle of poverty was to work our way up and send our kids to college. That's the trap most poor people get themselves into. It's easier for a person to just escape, to get out of poverty, than to change the situation."[1]

He had reached a turning point. But with his move to a neighborhood that ironically told its residents that they must try to leave, Chavez would find the people and the philosophies to, indeed, "change the situation."

EDUCATION AND FATHER DONALD MCDONNELL

From an unexpected knock on the door, Chavez opened himself to a new world of learning. A young Catholic priest named Father Donald McDonnell was making his rounds of the shacks in Sal Si Puedes, checking on the new arrivals in the barrio, asking them to gather together in his open-air meetings.

A graduate of St. Patrick's Seminary and University in Menlo Park, California, McDonnell was an expert linguist who spoke English, Spanish, Chinese, Japanese, German, and Portuguese. He had come from San Francisco where, from a church in a Mexican American community along Washington Street, he had begun to establish close ties to the migrant workers.

As a pastor at Saint Joseph's Church, McDonnell had helped form a neighborhood organization to foster strong cultural ties and to keep community and religious traditions alive. McDonnell had even helped the neighborhood form its own credit union, a major step for the community to pull together their meager earnings and help members secure loans. At a time when speaking any language other than English was discouraged and when pressures to abandon Mexican traditions was increasing, he and the other members worked avidly to ensure that they all lived up to the organization's motto "*Fe, Amistad y Progreso* ... Faith, Friendship, and Progress."

Now, McDonnell had traveled to Sal Si Puedes to help establish the same kind of mission church and community organization among the farm laborers that he had engineered among poor Mexican Americans in San Francisco.

For Chavez, the encounter with O'Donnell had profound implications. They were nearly the same age, both brimming with enthusiasm for changing the social order. McDonnell's ideas about applying basic Catholic doctrine toward help for migrants and others suffering social injustice mesmerized Chavez. "Father McDonnell sat with me past midnight telling me about social justice and the Church's stand on farm labor and reading from the encyclicals of Pope Leo XIII in which he upheld labor unions. I would do anything to get the Father to tell me more about labor history."[2]

Chavez began to accompany McDonnell to the labor camps to help with mass and even to the city jail to spend time with the prisoners. McDonnell became to Chavez tutor, friend, and fellow social worker. "We were some of the first members that joined his congregation for masses in a little Puerto Rican hall that was just a broken-down little shack," Chavez later remembered, "We became great friends when I began to help him, doing a little carpentry work, cleaning up the place, getting some chairs, and painting some old benches. I also drove for him and helped him recite mass."[3]

When McDonnell emphasized to Chavez that part of the responsibility of the Church and those who worked as its counselors was to administer to the physical nourishment as well as the spiritual, Cesar saw the outlines of his own thinking about religion and its place in his life. Listening to McDonnell relate the real problems of the field laborers to the teachings of the church, Chavez felt his life's lessons melding into a larger theme. McDonnell's talk about Mexican Americans organizing themselves to confront labor conditions head-on was much the same as the talk he had heard from his father and others in his family.

It was coming together, now, the lessons from his father about not accepting as fate the conditions in which you find yourself and about working with others in unions to improve those conditions; the teachings of his grandmother about spirituality; and the example of his mother, who, on many occasions, asked her children to go out by the railroad tracks and ask a hobo to come for dinner. The road for the Mexican American community of workers was not passively to accept their conditions as little more than slave labor, but to band themselves together as a family to work as a force for change.

McDonnell helped open up for Chavez a love of learning. Still only in his early twenties, Chavez already had experienced a full portion of rigorous work, had felt full blast the fury of prejudice and intolerance, and had within him the spirit to fight. Now, he would feed his ravenous need to know more, to put that experience in context. McDonnell became his guide to this new world of enlightenment.

"Actually," Chavez later said, "my education started when I met Father Donald McDonnell.... We had long talks about farm workers. I knew a lot about the work, but I didn't know anything about economics, and I learned quite a bit from him. He had a picture of a worker's shanty and a picture of a grower's mansion; a picture of a labor camp and a picture of a high-priced building in San Francisco owned by the same grower. When things were pointed out to me, I began to see.... Everything he said was aimed at ways to solve the injustice." Chavez read the papal encyclicals on labor and the writings of St. Francis of Assisi, an Italian monk who lived from 1182 to 1226 and devoted his life to helping the poor. "I began to grow and to see a lot of things that I hadn't seen before," he said. "My eyes opened, and I paid more attention to political and social events."[4]

He read biographies of labor organizers such as John L. Lewis and Eugene V. Debs and the history of the Knights of Labor. He read transcripts of U.S. Senate hearings on the plight of American workers that McDonnell had obtained. He read about the organization of unions and about strikes and the tactics used by corporate interests to break them. He read about the capitalist system, about the financing of large businesses, and about the vested interests that worked to the disadvantage of the common laborer.

Chavez also read Louis Fisher's *The Life of Gandhi*. The exposure to the life and teachings of Gandhi, the Indian politician and spiritual leader who had passed away in 1948, opened his eyes to the ways in which the poor in all countries and cultures can work together to improve their lives. The ideas of Gandhi, who preached and practiced the philosophy of nonviolent social change, would change Chavez's life.

About the same time Chavez was beginning his educational exploration, another slightly younger man across the country was finishing his own studies. After graduating from Morehouse College and finishing work at Crozer Theological Seminary, Martin Luther King Jr., the son of a Baptist preacher from Atlanta, Georgia, was completing his graduate work at Boston University. King was also becoming an ardent admirer of Gandhi's teachings on nonviolence as a road to social change. At that time in their lives, neither King nor Chavez had an appreciation of where that road might lead.

GANDHI AND NONVIOLENT PROTEST

Mohandas Gandhi, born in Gujarat, India, in 1869 into a business community family, studied law in England. In 1893, he arrived in South Africa on behalf of a client. Gandhi dressed in typical British attire. Nevertheless, while attempting to travel in the first-class compartment of a train reserved for whites only, he was forcibly removed for violating the segregation policies of the railroad. As Chavez read the biography of Gandhi, he thought of the incident in Delano several years earlier in which he had suffered similar treatment, being thrown out of a theater for violating its segregated seating policies.

Gandhi responded to the injustice by launching a movement for civil rights in South Africa and succeeded in changing some of the laws. When he returned to India in 1915, it was to a hero's welcome.

While in South Africa, Gandhi had developed a philosophy for challenging the social and political order through nonviolent protest. He began to challenge fellow Indians to adopt similar methods to confront their own political and social subjugation by the British in India. In 1920 Gandhi became the leader of Indian National Congress, a political organization, founded in 1885, dedicated to achieving for Indians a larger role in the making of British policy for India.

He began to live an ascetic life of prayer, fasting, and meditation. No longer did the studious lawyer dress in the style of whites; he now put on the simple, plain loincloth robes of an Indian farmer and subsisted on vegetables, fruit juices, and goat's milk. He built an ashram, a communal retreat, in which everyone in it shared equally in the household tasks, even cleaning the toilet, which according to Indian customs was the job reserved only for the lowest of classes. The philosophy he was demonstrating in this highly visible and personal way was that all people must be treated equally. Even when traveling back to England as head of the Indian National Congress, he continued to wear the plain garments. He drew astonished attention from his diplomatic counterparts and extensive comment from the British press, much of it derisive.

Nevertheless, he did have their attention and he began to speak of the injustices endured by the lower classes of Indian society and the subservient role into which Indian peoples had been reduced by British rule. His call was for Indians to resist British control through nonviolent opposition. Nothing could be gained by forceful revolution, he said, but the yoke of oppression could be lifted by large-scale noncooperation by a united Indian society. He advised Indians to boycott British-made garments and taught many the art of cotton spinning. He told them not to attend British universities, as he had done. He told them to refuse to follow British customs. The goal was to hurt the British occupiers economically and to overwhelm military might by the sheer force of numbers of resisters. Through nonviolent protest, Gandhi held, the British would eventually consider violence useless and would eventually leave India. Gandhi became the international symbol of a free India.

As he read of Gandhi's life and philosophy, Chavez was particularly struck by the power unleashed strategically by the nonviolent protests. Repeatedly, Gandhi organized campaigns of civil disobedience; many times he was arrested. In response to his arrests, he often fasted.

In 1930 Gandhi called on the Indian population to refuse to pay taxes, particularly the tax on salt. He organized a massive, 24-day march to the sea, in which thousands of Indians followed Gandhi from Ahmedabad to the Arabian Sea. There, he made salt by evaporating seawater. Once again arrested, he was released in 1931 with the British making concessions on their taxing policies.

Chavez later wrote,

> Gandhi described his tactics as moral jujitsu—always hitting the position off-balance, but keeping his principles His tactics of civil disobedience haven't hit this country on a massive scale, but they will.... Look what happened with Gandhi's salt march and the civil disobedience that followed after it He boycotted the salt so the government couldn't collect the tax, but then he showed the people how to make their own salt He boycotted clothes coming in from England, but he turned around and showed the Indians how to make their own clothes.[5]

Through Gandhi, Chavez would come to see nonviolence as both the philosophical and theological basis of his own commitment to social change. He would urge migrant workers to unleash the power of nonviolent resistance as a weapon against discrimination and inequality. In the years ahead, the young Mexican American organizer from California would apply the teachings of the celebrated Indian leader and philosopher to his own work. In the barrios and fields of California, the words and actions so familiar in Gandhi's career would become familiar—nonviolence, civil disobedience, boycott, strike, protest march, and fasting.

The writings and teachings of Gandhi and others had broadened his intellectual scope. For Chavez, however, the references to the workers and the poor were not abstractions. In those sun-baked fields he had worked beside them as one of them. Nearly two decades later, when he wrote a letter on behalf of migrant workers, it was one of personal testimony: "We are men and women who have suffered and endured much not only because of our abject poverty, but because we have been kept poor. The colors of our skins, the languages of our cultural and native origins, the lack of formal education, the exclusion from the democratic process, the numbers of our slain in recent wars—all these burdens generation after generation have sought to demoralize us, to break our human spirit, but God knows we are not agricultural implements or rented slaves, we are men."[6]

NOTES

1. Kim Benita Furumoto, "Viva La Causa! Cesar Chavez Remembered," *Diatribe*, May 1993, http://www.sfsu.edu/~cecipp/cesar_chavez/remembered.htm.

2. Ed Schwartz, "Cesar Chavez: Leader as Organizer," http://www.iscv.org/Opportunity/CesarChavez/cesarchavez.html.

3. Jacques Levy, Cesar Chavez: *Autobiography of La Causa*, http://chavez.cde.ca.gov/ModelCurriculum/Teachers/Lessons/Resources/Documents/Chavez_Biography_by_Levy.PDF

4. Cletus E. Daniel, "Cesar Chavez and the Unionization of California Farm Workers," in *Labor Leaders in America*, edited by Melvyn Dubofsky and Warren Van Tine (Urbana: University of Illinois Press, 1987), 350–365.

5. Levy.

6. Schwartz.

Chapter 3

COMMUNITY ORGANIZER

"I learned quite a bit from studying Gandhi, but the first practical steps I learned from the best organizer I know, Fred Ross. I first met him in Sal Si Puedes. He changed my life."[1]

For Cesar Chavez, the move to Sal Si Puedes was a turning point. There, he had met Father Donald McDonnell, who had not only introduced him to a life of learning Chavez had never before experienced but had involved him closely in his own work with the Mexican American community. It was in also in Sal Si Puedes that Chavez met Fred Ross.

In the spring of 1952, Chavez returned home one evening and heard from Helen that a white man wanted to see him. Chavez was suspicious, he remembered later. About the only whites who wanted to see Mexican Americans, he said, were contractors trying to hire them for stoop labor, or the police inquiring into crime matters, or sociologists from the University of California, Stanford University, or other academic institutions studying them to see how they lived—from family relationships to the ways in which they prepared their food. Chavez wanted no part of him.

Nevertheless, the man returned the next day. As Chavez watched from the window of his brother's house across the street, a very tall, thin fellow, dressed in old and worn clothes, got out of his car, accidentally banged his knee on the door, and limped toward the Chavez house. Helen, who thought the man might have something serious to discuss, pointed out Richard's house. Thus, a reluctant Chavez met Fred Ross.

About 20 years older than Chavez, he introduced himself and Chavez found himself listening. Ross had graduated from the University of Southern California in 1937 with the intention of becoming a classroom teacher. When he could find no teaching jobs available in the middle of the Depression, he found a job managing a federal migratory labor camp called Sunset, near Bakersfield, California.

When the acclaimed novelist John Steinbeck wrote *Grapes of Wrath* in 1939, a riveting story of the tribulations of the Joad family, a group of migrants from Oklahoma who traveled west to California looking for a way out of destitution, he modeled a labor camp in the novel after the Sunset Camp. Ross ran the camp shortly after Steinbeck left the area. About the same time Ross began to work at Sunset, an 11-year-old boy from Yuma, Arizona, began following the migrant trails of California with his parents. Like the Joads, the Chavez family worked the fields and vineyards of the San Joaquin Valley.

At the camp in Bakersfield, confronting the poverty and deplorable working conditions facing the workers, Ross decided to do something about them. His heart was in organizing. He earned the trust and respect of the migrants by instituting a form of self-government for the camp.

Every day he went from cabin to cabin encouraging residents to band together as a large force to help improve the conditions and to fight for concessions from those who held power. He prodded people to speak up for their interests, to fight in spite of their fear of confrontation, and to be heard.

When Ross left the migrant camp, it was to take on another organizing project. Joining the American Friends Service Committee, he worked up and down the West Coast to help Japanese Americans who had been herded into internment camps during World War II find jobs.

Following the war, he returned to Southern California and joined with social activists in helping blacks and Mexican Americans fight against segregation in housing and education. In Arizona, Ross helped Yaqui Indians acquire medical facilities, streets, and other basic needs.

And now, Ross was in Sal Si Puedes and, not surprisingly, had become a close friend of Father McDonnell. He was representing the Community Service Organization (CSO), a social service group that was founded in Los Angeles in 1947.

As did other Mexican American community organizations, or *mutualistas*, the CSO promoted self-reliance and provided a variety of services, including low-cost medical care and job referral. It acted to help ensure that children of Mexican descent receive a decent education and it worked for civil rights issues. CSO was also active in encouraging Mexican Americans to vote.

Ross, who was learning Spanish from flash cards, met small groups of Mexican Americans in their homes. The groups then branched out into the community, creating new groups and establishing footholds. The Los Angeles CSO became highly successful in registering new voters and in establishing citizen involvement in social issues.

Ross explained to Chavez that the CSO was organizing chapters in a number of other California localities, one of which was the San Jose area, home to Sal Si Puedes. The CSO, Ross predicted, would soon be a forceful Mexican American civil rights organization in California.

Although Chavez was at first dubious, he agreed to hold a house meeting with Ross for some of his friends. "I invited some of the rougher guys I knew and bought some beer," Chavez remembered. "We'd let him speak a while and when I gave them a signal, shifting my cigarette from my right hand to the left, we'd tell him off and run him out of the house."[2]

When Ross began speaking, it did not take long for Chavez, who had a canny instinct for judging people and their motives, to make a decision. There would be no cigarette signals this night. Although he did not learn that first night about all of the earlier efforts Ross had made on behalf of minority communities, Chavez saw quickly that here was a man whose life's calling was to work for those who were struggling and in need. He also sensed that the kind of approach described by Ross could build power.

When Ross asked him to join in the work, Chavez accepted. That night in his journal, Ross wrote, "I think I found the guy I'm looking for."[3]

ON THE ROAD FOR THE CSO

Seizing the opportunity, Chavez was at once enthusiastic and wary. Although he captured the loyalty of friends and small of groups of people with whom he associated, he had no experience in speaking publicly to groups, was unsure about his organizing abilities, and somewhat frightened about the responsibilities that were to be directed to him. Nevertheless, he vigorously leaped into the work with a dedication and loyalty that was infectious. He later wrote, "I tagged along to every one of Fred's house meetings during that first campaign in San Jose—sometimes two a night. The thing I liked most about Fred was there were ... no pretensions, no ego gimmicks. Just plain hard work, at times grinding work."[4]

"I was very much impressed with Cesar," Ross remembered. "I could tell he was intensely interested, a kind of burning interest rather than one of those inflammatory things that lasts one night and is then forgotten. He asked many questions, part of it to see if I really knew, putting me to the test. But it was much more than that." Ross also discovered that Chavez was an exceedingly quick study: "He understood it almost immediately, as soon as I drew the picture. He got the point—the whole question of power and the development of power within the group. He made the connections very quickly between the civic weakness of the group and the social neglect in the barrio, and also conversely, what could be done about that social neglect once the power was developed." Ross said that in one two-month stretch, Chavez was the only worker that came out every night.[5]

During the day, Chavez would pick apricots; at night he conducted house meetings and talked with fellow migrants about their constitutional rights and showed them how to register to vote. So pleased was Ross with the progress that Chavez made early on that he turned over control of the San Jose drive to him. "He looked to me like potentially the best grass roots leader I'd ever run into," said Ross.[6]

The young organizer wasted no time in bringing his own tactics to the job. Instead of relying mostly on college students to serve as registrars for the voting drive campaign, Chavez recruited his friends from the barrio. By the end of the campaign he had produced several thousand new voters.

Besides the organizing experience he gained in the voter registration drive in San Jose, Chavez also got a rough dose of the vicious, partisan politics of the early 1950s. These new voters that Chavez and his team had signed up threatened the local Republican Party's control of the area. Fearing this new Mexican American voting bloc arising in its midst, the Republican Central Committee decided to challenge first-time Mexican American voters at the polls. The Republicans showed up on election day questioning whether the voters were illegal aliens or whether they had criminal backgrounds. It was a blatant effort to intimidate voters, many of whom were at the polls for the first time in their lives.

The tactics so infuriated Ross that, on behalf of the CSO, he wired the U.S. Attorney General in Washington. Chavez added his name to the letter. For the Federal Bureau of Investigation (FBI) and for other law enforcement agencies, this letter presented a new target of investigation. The target, unhappily for the CSO, was not the possible voter intimidation but the CSO itself. Could this new organization in San Jose and its leaders, including Cesar Chavez, be tied in some way to an anti-American conspiracy?

These were the early days of the Cold War, of an escalating fear of the domination of the Soviet Union and of communist infiltration not only in American society but in the highest echelons of government. The junior senator from Wisconsin, Joseph McCarthy, claimed to have lists of high-ranking public officials secretly allied with the communist party.

Government leaders and the media talked of the threat of nuclear weapons and the uncharted horrors that could lie ahead. Americans engaged in civil defense drills and built homemade bomb shelters. They watched the U.S. Congress interrogate Americans about their possible links to communist groups. They watched as writers and Hollywood personalities were paraded before inquisitors. They read in magazines and newspapers about the progress being made to devise new chemical and biological weapons. They read of the dire prospects of the world's population doubling before the end of the century, bringing with it poverty, disease, and new recruits for the communist regimes. They wanted their government to protect them from this growing menace.

If traitors were infiltrating the nation's highest offices, if communist leaders around the globe were arming against and aiming at the United States, where was the real protection for the average citizen? Chavez remembered that in the late 1940s, his family had joined picketers in a strike against the DiGiorgio farming company. In Bakersfield, a young congressman from California organized hearings concerning labor walkouts. Chavez was so interested in the subject that he managed to listen in person to some of the deliberations. The congressman believed that the labor protestors were connected to a communist plot. The congressman was future president Richard Nixon.

And now, a few of the nation's defenders turned their attention to San Jose, California, and looked at a young, Mexican American farmworker who had just turned organizer. Who was this new face in the protester ranks? What were his links to the international communist menace?

"The FBI agents took me in their car for a meeting with members of the Republican Central Committee which turned into a shouting match," Chavez later remembered. "That's the first [time] I started shouting at Anglos, shouting back at them." The confrontation became the subject of a newspaper story and suddenly Chavez was the talk of the area. "The newspaper had a lot of influence during those McCarthy days. Anyone who organized or worked for civil rights was called a Communist. Anyone who talked about police brutality was called a Communist. Everywhere I went to organize they would bluntly ask, 'Are you a Communist?' I would answer, 'No.' "How do we know?' 'You don't know. You know because I tell you.' And we would go around and around on that ... Later I found out that when they learned I was close to the church, they wouldn't question me so much. So I'd get the priests to come out and give me their blessing."[7]

Over the years, the file on Cesar Chavez at the FBI in Washington, D.C., would grow larger and larger. It included information about his movements, his friends, his correspondence, his plans, his speeches, his philosophy, and his family. In its continuing and intensive surveillance of Chavez, the FBI would find no evidence of his being implicated in communist activities. The massive file, instead, filled up with evidence of the remarkably active work and strong commitment of Chavez on behalf of Mexican Americans.

After the highly successful drive in San Jose in 1952, Ross and the other leaders of CSO decided to hire Chavez as a full-time organizer. His pay was $35 a week. In his entire career, he would never earn more than $6,000 a year.

Chavez's single-minded purpose soon became evident to all those small groups of people he gathered in the house meetings and to those fellow workers whom he recruited and who stayed with him over years of work. Helen encouraged him, remaining steadfastly behind the cause that drove them both, even though his immersion in his work left little time to help raise the children. They would number eight in all. Their third child, Linda, was born in 1951, Eloise in 1952, Anna in 1953, Paul in 1957, Elizabeth in 1958, and Anthony, also in 1958. If some of the children would harbor resentment at his continued absences from home, if he gave up many of the joys of a personal life, Chavez considered this work of helping the poor his calling. For that calling, he would sacrifice.

"He was smarter and nicer and more charismatic and cuter" than the rest of the early leadership, said one of the early workers. Soft-spoken and with a gentle expression to his face, he had a leader's great gift for connecting with individuals personally. "When he talked to you," a former aide recalled, "he let you know you were the whole world for him."[8]

Throughout the 1950s, he would organize more than 20 new CSO chapters in such California towns as Madera, Bakersfield, and Hanford. His years with the CSO brought the young organizer into contact with a whole range of public and private authorities that were involved with labor issues, immigration, and social problems involving Mexican Americans. Chavez listened personally to their problems. They came to him singly or in groups. He would write letters to government agencies for them as well as intervene for them in misunderstandings with the police, with physicians, and with welfare department representatives. If Mexican Americans were tricked into fraudulent sales contracts, he would steer them through the bureaucratic maze. If their children were removed from school for discipline problems, he would try to help.

Although he had setbacks and disappointments, the unobtrusive-looking, boyish Chavez was making a mark. Throughout the agricultural regions of California, in towns like Buttonwillow and Wasco, Chavez moved with his family in the 1950s. In houses and clubs, he gathered workers together to talk about citizenship, voting, and the work of the CSO. He wrote to Ross from the town of Oildale just before Christmas in 1954, "Some of them thought the CSO was a fly-by-night deal and that it would die before it got started ... I explained to them that the CSO is an action group and not a talking one."[9] The young, aggressive organizer was gaining wide recognition and respect. And seeing what he was willing to do for them, the workers were quickly rallying to do what they could for the CSO.

In the mid-1950s, Chavez met Dolores Huerta, a vigorous, attractive associate of Fred Ross and the mother of seven children. At the Los Angeles headquarters, Huerta had heard of the organizing skills of Cesar Chavez, but after meeting him briefly she seemed unimpressed, remembering mostly his shyness. In 1957, they met again at a CSO meeting in Stockton. This time, she marveled at the way he answered questions directly, precisely, and without pretension. He was, she concluded, a special messenger and activist for the cause of the workers. Dolores Huerta would become a pivotal ally for Chavez in the coming years.

In August 1958, Chavez traveled to Oxnard, a leading citrus growing region north of Los Angeles, to establish a local office of the CSO. It was in Oxnard that Chavez worked against the bracero program, a federally funded effort of the federal government to bring laborers directly from Mexico to California to work in the fields during labor shortages. The growers exploited the braceros, housing them ill-maintained labor camps, paying them extremely low wages, and then sending them back to Mexico at the end of the harvest season. If the braceros complained about their working conditions, they were immediately deported.

Under the bracero program, growers throughout California were permitted under federal regulations to use Mexican workers only after exhausting the available pool of local farm workers. Because of the financial advantages that the bracero program afforded the growers, they often ignored those regulations. Thus, many of the local California Mexican American workers and other migrant laborers frequently went without jobs while growers brought in increasing numbers of braceros. By the late 1950s, Mexican American field workers had been to a large extent replaced by the braceros. The signs declaring "No Pickers Wanted" increasingly greeted those looking for work.

Although Chavez sympathized with the plight of the Mexican workers brought in to the United States in the harvest seasons and then sent back, he also saw the larger labor issues involved. Mexican American workers could not protest wages or working conditions for fear of losing jobs to braceros. The braceros, on the other hand, could not protest for fear of being returned immediately to Mexico.

For 13 months, Chavez and the CSO fought against these practices. He employed many of the nonviolent but aggressive tactics being used by Martin Luther King Jr. and others in the civil rights movement that was now gaining momentum in the American South. Civil rights organizers had used "sit-ins" at lunch counters to protest discrimination against blacks. In Oxnard, Chavez organized a sit-down strike in the fields to challenge the hiring practices.

He also put together a boycott of merchants who sold the products grown by the farmers who used bracero workers extensively. Workers under Chavez's leadership picketed and filed complaints with the federal and state government.

They carried on a march from the town to the fields, but not before Chavez had notified newspaper reporters and television stations that it was to take place. At a tomato ranch, 10 carloads of workers and their families gathered, singing a song about the Mexican folk hero, Pancho Villa, and carrying pictures of the Virgin of Guadalupe, whose image, it is said in Mexican culture, appeared on the cloak of an Aztec named Juan Diego in 1531. The Virgin of Guadalulpe, the patron and symbol of Mexico, representing the fusion of the Aztec and Spanish cultures, often appeared on flags carried by Chavez marchers.

The workers in Oxnard also began to keep records about specific hiring decisions that had violated the law. They even picketed a meeting of the U.S. secretary of labor, James Mitchell, when he visited the local area. They rallied the community so convincingly that, by the end of 1959, they had managed to set up at a local CSO headquarters a "hiring hall" through which most of the growers, weary from the struggle against Chavez and his lieutenants, had agreed to find workers. Chavez had essentially turned the local CSO in Oxnard into a union hall. It was in Oxnard that Chavez began to see clearly in his mind the exciting potential of organizing the farmworkers of California into a union.

Chavez had gathered to his cause in Oxnard more than 1,500 workers, most of them farm laborers. He saw the group that he had assembled there in the year and a half of work as the nucleus of a union that could use all the tools—the boycotts, marches, and strikes—he had employed against the bracero program. With seemingly indefatigable energy, he had given his all for the CSO. He wanted to take the gains, the resources, and the experience of Oxnard and turn the CSO into a farmworkers' union. He believed that the workers needed to establish formal contracts with the growers in order to keep the gains they had achieved. With no formal union contracts,

Chavez knew, the growers, in future years, could return to the system that had so hurt Mexican American farm laborers.

Encouraged by the backing of the 1,500 workers at Oxnard, he proposed to the CSO that they found a union. The proposal was turned down. The organization, the CSO Board of Directors insisted, was by nature a social service program and civic organization, not a union. Their work was community self-help, not labor relations. Despite the setback, Chavez had achieved such respect and support among the management of the CSO that he was promoted to be its executive director in 1959.

Chavez continued to work for the CSO until 1962. Three months before its annual convention in the spring of 1962 in the Imperial Valley desert town of Calexico, Chavez once again asked CSO's board members if he could establish a pilot project to organize a union of farmworkers. He would take no salary from the CSO itself but would accept funds from the workers. The Board of Directors agreed to this plan upon the condition that a majority of the full membership give its support at the annual convention.

In Calexico, Chavez and the organization to which he had devoted himself for a decade came to a crossroads. When his proposal was presented to the full membership for vote, it was a moment of high tension. Most of the members voted not to support Chavez in his effort to make a fundamental change of direction in the organization. They wanted the focus of the CSO to remain as a civic organization serving the interests of Mexican Americans, principally in the cities. Although the members had great respect and admiration for Chavez and what he had accomplished, they did not want to turn the organization into a union.

When the vote was announced, Chavez quietly rose in the hall and said that he had an announcement. It was two words—"I resign." Although his resignation turned the convention into near-bedlam and although several shaken members tried to persuade Chavez to reconsider, he did not retreat from his decision. "It took me six months to get over leaving CSO," he said later.[10]

On March 31, 1962, his thirty-fifth birthday, Chavez cleared out his desk at the CSO headquarters in Los Angeles. With Helen and the children, he drove to the small beach town of Carpinteria, near Santa Barbara. While the children frolicked in the sand, the couple talked of their plans. They would go to Delano to start a union. It was true that they had little money, no property, and no promise of work. Nevertheless, it was Helen's hometown. Two of her sisters lived in Delano and two brothers were nearby. It was also the town that Chavez's brother, Richard, had made his home. There was no better place than Delano, they agreed, to chase a dream. After filling the tank of the battered Mercury, they headed north.

NOTES

1. Jacques Levy, *Cesar Chavez: Autobiography of La Causa*, http://chavez. cde.ca.gov/ModelCurriculum/Teachers/Lessons/Resources/Documents/Chavez_ Biography_by_Levy.PDF.

2. Richard del Castillo and Richard Garcia, *Cesar Chavez: A Triumph of Spirit* (Norman: University of Oklahoma Press, 1995), 25.

3. "UFW Memorial Honors Lifelong Activist," *Los Angeles Times,* 19 October 1992, p. 3.

4. Ibid.

5. Levy.

6. "A Farm-Bred Unionist: Cesar Chavez," *New York Times,* 11 March 1968, p. 22.

7. Levy.

8. David Gates, "A Secular Saint of the '60s," *Newsweek* (3 May 1993), p. 68.

9. Susan Ferriss and Ricardo Sandoval, *The Fight in the Fields: Cesar Chavez and the Farmworkers Movement* (Orlando, FL: Paradigm Productions, Inc., 1997), 52.

10. Ibid., 62.

Chapter 4

THE RISE OF THE BLACK EAGLE

Soft-spoken, with heavy-lidded eyes and an occasional wry grin, he was 35 years old when he arrived in Delano with his family in the spring of 1962. With a shock of coal-black hair sweeping across his broad face, he seemed almost boyish, his peaceful demeanor and quiet voice masking a fiery spirit. In measured tones, he talked about upsetting the established order. He had a natural sense of community, gathering around him a harvest of loyal friends who trusted him, sensed his roots and purpose. However unlikely it seemed, Cesar Chavez was a man ready to make a difference.

"A big job has to be done and we know it," he said. "It will take many years. But, we know that a union of farm workers is going to be built somehow because the workers are on the move, and they want a union."[1]

A town of twelve thousand in 1962, Delano was in the center of the nation's table grape industry. Harboring no illusions, Chavez knew that rounding up supporters for a full-scale union would be difficult and slow. Most labor leaders privately believed that Chavez's goal of creating the first successful union of farmworkers in U.S. history was close to impossible.

Farm laborers presented a union organizer with a number of seemingly overwhelming hurdles. The workers were largely illiterate, extremely poor, and divided culturally from mainstream America. They did not usually remain very long in one locality, making stability and communication highly dubious. They had, up to this point, little economic power. If they refused to work, growers could replace them with cheaper bracero labor.

If Chavez was to create enough support to start a union movement, he would also have to overcome a problem of expectations. First, the workers themselves had endured the injustices so long and knew the reprisals that had been dealt to others who had challenged the system that they expected the treatment and the system to continue. On the other side, the growers and the rest of the community also fully expected the system to continue as it had. Workers knew their place and did the work they were expected to perform; if not, all the local institutions, from the police to business owners and political leaders—could be expected to react defensively, protecting the status quo and what they considered the usual way of doing things.

Using the family's life savings of about $1,200, small gifts and loans from some friends and relatives, and the wages that Helen was able to earn by returning to work in the fields, Chavez began the painstaking groundwork of building an association of farmworkers. As he began to make the rounds of Delano and nearby fruit growing areas, he moved slowly in introducing the idea of a union. He avoided using the term because to most of the workers union meant "strikes," through which some of them had already suffered. Strikes had, in some cases, brought higher paychecks, they knew, but in most they had meant layoffs and, sometimes, violence. Instead, Chavez began simply to earn the confidence and trust of the people and began to organize them into a community service group much like those he formed for the CSO.

From one farm labor camp to another, he worked the San Joaquin Valley. He talked about the potential strengths of a social movement or *movimiento* and spread the idea that to gain real power, the workers must consolidate and, through confrontational tactics, use whatever nonviolent muscle they had.

One of the men later said, "Here was Cesar burning with a patient fire, poor like us, dark like us ... moving people to talk about their problems, attacking the little problems first, and suggesting always, suggesting never more solutions that seemed attainable. We didn't know it until we met him, but he was the leader we had been waiting for."[2]

Julio Hernandez, a cotton field worker, lived in nearby Cocoran. He was one of the field workers who had earlier had an unfortunate experience involving a union organizer who had offered him support and had abandoned him at the time of a strike. He had, for a time, been blacklisted, refused work by the local growers because of that union incident. At first, Hernandez did not want to have anything to do with Chavez. When Chavez called at his house, Hernandez was out playing pool. When a friend went to the pool hall to tell him that Chavez was at his house,

Hernandez kept on playing pool. He did not return that night until two o'clock in the morning. Chavez was still there.

For three hours, until five o'clock, Chavez, Hernandez, and Hernandez's wife, Josephina, listened to the young organizer quietly weave his usual "house meeting" magic. Hernandez joined up with Chavez. He found himself delivering leaflets in the early morning hours before work. His wife and daughter became directly involved in the organization. They would remain loyal workers for the cause.

By the fall of 1962, Chavez had not only lined up workers who were interested in joining the union, he also had drawn to his side other loyal and talented lieutenants.

DOLORES HUERTA AND THE "CO-FANATICS"

If Chavez himself was an unlikely leader, his principal ally experienced a similarly unusual rise to prominence. Born in 1930 in Dawson, New Mexico, a small mining town, Dolores Huerta came from a family that had to struggle for survival. Her father, Juan Fernandez, was a miner and her mother was a cannery worker and cook. When Huerta was six, her parents divorced and her mother moved the children to Stockton, California, where, through determination and grit, she managed to run a boardinghouse for farm laborers. Generous with workers down on their luck, she helped instill in Dolores the same kind of respect for the poor that Chavez's own parents had instilled in him.

At the age of 20, Dolores married a manual laborer named Ralph Head, took on a number of clerical jobs, and began taking night courses at Stockton College in hopes of becoming a teacher. The marriage soon ended.

After completing her college work for a teaching certificate, Huerta took a job at a local grammar school, but soon became disillusioned with trying to work with children who had come to school hungry and without shoes. She soon decided that she could do more for them by engaging in social work and in organizing farmworkers to ensure that those children no longer had to walk around shoeless and hungry. She married Ventura Huerta, with whom she had five children and whose name she took for her own.

Like Chavez, Huerta became a recruit of Fred Ross. She met him in Fresno in 1955. She later remembered Ross showing her pictures of the workers in Los Angeles whom he had helped mobilize. She remembered the excitement of learning about the health clinics that the CSO had helped build in the city and the fact that a number of local Hispanic leaders active in CSO had actually entered the political arena. She wanted to be a part of it.

In Stockton she became a key CSO organizer, putting aside questions about why a woman with a growing family would place herself in the middle of activity that was usually a province of men. Attractive, dynamic, full of enthusiasm that could rouse the lethargic to action, Huerta took on the work of the CSO with a passion Ross had seldom observed.

She helped run the CSO civic and educational programs in Stockton. Soon, she was taking an active political role for the organization, pressing local government leaders for improvements in the barrio. She also traveled for the CSO to Sacramento to help lobby state government leaders. Her increasing activism took a toll on her marriage to Huerta, who felt that she should be at home with the children. The two later divorced.

In 1959 Huerta was involved in an effort by the AFL-CIO to organize a farmworkers' union. The infant group was called the Agricultural Workers Organizing Committee (AWOC) and it made enough progress to attempt a few strikes against growers in the Imperial Valley in the early 1960s. Nevertheless, Huerta, who acted for a time as the committee's secretary-treasurer, soon became unhappy with the organization, whose leaders, she thought, did not understand fully the needs of the farmworkers and who did not have the fire to take on the growers and their contractors. The migrant workforce, she realized, was easily intimidated and manipulated. It would take much more than the type of activity practiced by the AWOC to make an impact.

When Chavez met Huerta, they began a lifelong friendship, often turbulent, but always with shared ideals and goals. Huerta later said, "When Cesar told me, 'I'm going to start my own union,' I was just appalled, the thought was so overwhelming. But when the initial shock wore off, I thought it was exciting."[3]

Huerta followed Chavez out of the CSO and into his effort to organize a farmworkers' union. They decided to call for an organizational meeting to officially establish the new union.

On Sunday, September 30, 1962, in an abandoned theater in Fresno, California, approximately 200 workers gathered to show their solidarity. They called the new organization The National Farm Workers Association (NFWA). They adopted a union motto: *Viva la causa!* ("Long live the cause!"). They also waved a new flag bearing the organizational symbol—an Aztec eagle, emblematic of pride and dignity. A white circle in the flag signified the hopes and aspirations of the farm laborers; the black represented the plight of the workers; and the red background stood for the hard work and sacrifice that the union members would have to give. As Chavez's cousin, Manuel Chavez, who had worked on the design of the flag, pulled a cord to unveil it, he declared, "When that damn eagle flies, the problems of the farm workers will be over!"[4]

In his new plan of action delivered at the organizational meeting, Chavez talked about lobbying the governor's office for a minimum wage for farmworkers of $1.50 per hour and for the right to unemployment insurance. He talked about the possibility of collective bargaining, in which the association would approach the growers as a group to negotiate working conditions and pay, an unheard of proposition in California's migrant farm labor industry. He also talked about plans for an association-run credit union and a hiring hall to help workers locate jobs. In short, this was going to be a union. It was not called a union at first but it would be one. It would organize quietly in order to avoid frightening potential members who feared for their jobs and also to avoid active opposition from the growers. Dues would be $3.50 a month.

To *La Causa* rallied the so-called co-fanatics of the movement: In addition to Chavez, Dolores Huerta, and Julio Hernandez, there were Jim Drake and others of the California Migrant Ministry, a group of Protestant ministers dedicated to helping the farm workers. Chavez later recalled:

> We began to run into the California Migrant Ministry in the camps and field. They were about the only ones there, and a lot of us were very suspicious, since we were Catholics and they were Protestants. However, they had developed a very clear conception of the Church. It was called to serve, to be at the mercy of the poor, and not to try to use them. After a while this made a lot of sense to us, and we began to find ourselves working side by side with them.[5]

A graduate of Occidental College and Union Theological Seminary, Reverend Jim Drake was about to accept a pastoral position when he was approached by Chris Hartmire, a minister who was director of the California Migrant Ministry. The organization had decided to join Chavez's movement and Hartmire assigned Drake to assist in the organizational efforts. "Jim was not a big talker," Hartmire said. "He was believing and doing. He had this certainty about the rightness of the cause." This became quite clear when Drake openly criticized some ministers for what he regarded as timidity toward the growers. "All we're talking about is that some of you guys are going to lose your jobs," he said. "Two thousand farm workers have already lost theirs."[6]

When Chavez began his local tours, Reverend Drake was soon at his side: "Workers were not organized in dramatic meetings," Drake said, "but one by one, in a car on the way to a labor commissioner hearing, or while driving to meet an industrial accident referee." And while the new member drove, Drake said, Chavez would talk. Clearly and carefully, he would outline the plan. A growing number of farmworkers passed the word. If you have trouble, they were told, "Go to Delano, Chavez can help."[7]

Drake provided a vital connection for Chavez to the California Migrant Ministry. "Whatever the need was, Jim was there," Dolores Huerta said of Drake. "He had a very, very big heart."[8]

Chavez was emotionally moved by the relationship of these ministers in Drake's organization to the farm laborers. He often used the example of this group to persuade other religious organizations, including the Catholic Church, to send more representatives to the fields and barrios. For his entire career, Chavez would enjoy strong ecumenical support for the movement.

Gilbert Padilla, like Huerta and Chavez, was another CSO veteran. Padilla's earliest days were in the fields. Born in a migrant labor camp, raised alongside his mother, whose fiery indignation against injustice fueled his own, Padilla and his five brothers served in World War II. When they returned home and sought jobs in the fields they had worked before the war, the foreman tried to pay them less money than they had received before their service in the military. Indignant, they left.

Padilla began to express his resentment against the system by joining the CSO. And now, with Chavez, he was ready to strike bigger blows.

At a constitutional convention held in Fresno on January 21, 1963, Chavez was elected president of the new organization; Dolores Huerta, Julio Hernandez, and Gilbert Padilla became vice presidents. The preamble to the Constitution that Chavez had drafted at a table in his garage made clear the abuses against which the movement would march:

We the Farm Workers of America, have tilled the soil, sown the seeds and harvested the crops. We have provided food in abundance for the people in the cities, and the nation and world but have not had sufficient food to feed our own children.

While industrial workers, living and working in one place, have joined together and grown strong, we have been isolated, scattered and hindered from uniting our forces.[9]

INFANT STEPS

In the formative months and years of the National Farm Workers Association, the union leaders fanned out across the farm areas of California and slowly gained recruits. Chavez and Drake held town meetings. Huerta began to take charge of administrative matters. Padilla took jobs picking cherries and peeling peaches so he could secretly pass out cards to workers in the fields. Manuel Chavez, a vigorous organizer, decided to give up a permanent, well-paying job as a car dealer in San Diego to join his cousin and his cause.

Nevertheless, progress was painstakingly slow. Workers would agree to join and then change their minds. Many were not in the area long enough to be of any help to the union. For the organization's leaders, finding ways to feed their families and, at the same time, tend to an infant union became next to impossible.

Some members of the CSO and the California Migrant Ministry began to send small contributions. The overwhelming weight of the effort, however, rested with the few leaders who worked in the fields during the day and spent long evenings at banged-up typewriters producing flyers or meeting with workers in their homes. "There were times, of course, when we didn't know whether we'd survive," Chavez said. "We'd get members, and then they would drop out. We might go all day collecting dues and then have every single one say, 'I can't pay. I'm sorry, but I don't want to belong any more.'"[10]

"The main thing in convincing someone," Chavez observed, "is to spend time with him. It doesn't matter if he [can't] read, write, or even speak well. What is important is that he is a man and second that he has shown some initial interest. One good way to develop leadership is to take a man with you in your car. And it works a lot better if you're doing the driving, that way you are in charge. You drive, he sits there, and you talk."[11]

He found it relatively easy to interest workers in the idea of the association, he later recalled. It was important, however, to find out as early as possible which people might truly be committed and willing to work over a long period. "You build a core of people who keep coming back to talk. You find certain people who are respected as leaders in every community; and you find that some of these leaders are committed to the task ahead. A union, then, is not simply getting enough workers to stage a strike. A union is building a group with a spirit and an existence all its own."[12]

Often, Chavez would be on the road in the middle of the night heading for work sites. Chavez's own children, as well as his nephews and nieces, all pitched in to help as the registration drive mounted. On some occasions he would squeeze his eight children into his battered station wagon and try to make the trips a family outing. All of them looked forward to ice cream after the long hot rides.

He kept up a steady stream of short letters to Fred Ross about the union's progress. At times, the overwhelming, self-imposed schedule would find

Chavez weary and slightly discouraged. At other times, he was almost giddy at the progress, talking about the hopeful looks on the faces of workers as they signed the union's little white registration cards.

By 1964, the NFWA had signed up more than 1,000 families. For the first time, Chavez could go on a salary from union dues. The organization had launched a credit union, run by Helen, and other community service programs such immigration counseling and assistance with voter registration.

The organization was also able to begin publishing its farm work newspaper called *El Malcriado* (meaning the ill-bred or misfit). Through its pages, workers could follow the cartoon figure Don Sotaco as he surveyed the area scene regarding jobs, calls for higher wages, and issues involving worker conditions. The little publication was irreverent, both funny and angry, and brought the issues vividly to light, even for those who were relatively illiterate. Eventually published in both Spanish and English and available at barrio grocery stores, the newspaper became another source of unity around which the new movement could communicate and build enthusiasm.

A few years after the formation of the union, a newspaper reporter asked Chavez to explain the energy and conviction that he had brought to this Herculean task, one that was on its face nearly laughable in its chances for success. Chavez simply said, "For many years I was a farm worker, a migratory worker, and, well, personally, and I'm being very frank, maybe it's just a matter of trying to even the score, you know."[13]

WHEN TO STRIKE

Although the NFWA had made substantial progress by 1965, Chavez was not yet planning a major strike. The power of the growers and affiliated companies represented a formidable adversary. Chavez figured it would take at least another couple of years for the union to have the money, the numbers of members, and the experience necessary to take on that kind of power.

Faced with demands by workers, Chavez knew, the companies would employ a number of ruthless strikebreaking strategies that the union would have to overcome. They would approach the courts for rulings to prevent the union from boycotting or picketing. They would hire "goons" from other parts of the valley to come in and beat up strikers. They would bring in undocumented foreign workers to help to replace picketing workers. They would enlist the efforts of police to arrest picketers and protesters for causing mayhem. They would plant stories in the media that the strikers were violent, un-American, and probably communists. Chavez knew well the tactics he would face and was gearing up his own forces to take on the challenge. The time to strike, he believed, was not yet at hand.

As Chavez knew, however, events often change plans. In the spring of 1965, he suddenly found himself in the middle of a small strike that broke out among 85 workers at a McFarland, California, rose farm called Mount Arbor. Aware of the growing influence of the NFWA, the flower workers approached Chavez for help in gaining a wage increase. Both Chavez and Huerta, without deeply involving the NFWA, worked for several days helping to prepare the workers for the strike. Their efforts were successful, at least in the short run. The growers agreed to a wage increase but not to any long-term guarantees. Nevertheless, on the front page of *El Malcriado*, the union proclaimed victory in the "War of the Roses."

In the summer, migrant workers in Porterville, California, went on a strike to protest an increase in rents in farmworker camps. The Tulane County Housing Authority decided to raise the rent on veritable tin shacks in the labor camp to $25 a month. Although the NFWA remained largely on the sidelines, Gil Padilla and Jim Drake actively worked on behalf of the strikers, as did others involved with the Migrant Ministry. Chavez later remembered that it was at the rent strike that the NFWA first flew the colors of the NFWA black eagle at a strike. Again, the strikers achieved victory. The tin shacks were demolished and replaced by small cottages.

At the end of the summer of 1965, grapes were ripening in the fields of Chavez's home base of Delano. Grape pickers were expected to work in the vineyards for 90 cents an hour plus 10 cents a basket. Working conditions in the camps and fields were miserable. Emboldened by the talk of strikes and the small successes they had seen in California earlier in the year, workers demanded a pay raise to $1.25 cents an hour. The growers refused. The stage was set for a drama that Chavez himself could not have anticipated.

NOTES

1. "A Farm-Bred Unionist: Cesar Estrada Chavez," *New York Times*, 11 March, 1968, p. 22.

2. Dick Meister, "'La Huelga' Becomes 'La Causa'," *New York Times Magazine* (17 November 1968), 52, 90.

3. M. Christie Mullikin and Carol Larson Jones, "Dolores Huerta: Cesar Chavez' Partner in Founding the United Farm Workers Union in California," http://www.csupomona.edu/~jis/1997/Mullikin.pdf.

4. Linda Altman, *Migrant Farm Workers: The Temporary People* (New York, Franklin Watts, 1994), 64.

5. Cesar E. Chavez: "The Mexican-American and the Church," 8–10 March 1968, http://www.americanrhetoric.com/speeches/chavezspeech.htm.

6. Douglas Martin, "Jim Drake, 63, an Organizer of Workers and a 60's Boycott, Dies," 9 September 2001, http://lists.village.virginia.edu/lists_archive/sixties-l/3507.html.

7. Altman, 62–63.

8. "A Rare, Unheralded Champion of American Workers," 22 February 2004, http://www.epinions.com/content_3786842244.

9. Altman, 66.

10. Richard del Castillo and Richard Garcia, *Cesar Chavez: A Triumph of Spirit* (Norman: University of Oklahoma Press, 1995), 38–39.

11. Ed Schwartz, "Cesar Chavez: Leader as Organizer," http://www.iscv.org/Opportunity/CesarChavez/cesarchavez.html.

12. "Viva la Causa: Cesar E. Chavez, Interviewed by Wendy Goepel," originally published in *Farm Labor* 1, no. 5 (April 1964), available at http://www.sfsu.edu/~cecipp/cesar_chavez/lacausa.htm.

13. "A Farm-Bred Unionist," *New York Times*, 3 March, 1968, p. 22.

Chapter 5

THE DELANO GRAPE STRIKE

A CALL FOR ACTION

On September 16, 1965, the membership of Cesar Chavez's farmworkers' union gathered at Our Lady of Guadalupe Church in Delano. It was Mexican Independence Day, honoring the time Mexicans achieved the end of Spanish colonial rule.

Into the pews and balconies wedged more than 500 excited workers and their families. Chavez had sent out word through local disc jockeys on Spanish radio and in the National Farm Workers Association (NFWA) paper that something big was in the works.

Eight days earlier, Filipino grape workers, led by Larry Itliong of the Agricultural Workers Organizing Committee (AWOC), went on strike against the Delano growers demanding higher wages, better living conditions, and fair hiring practices. The leaders had come to Chavez asking that his union, the NFWA, join the strike.

Although apprehensive about the readiness of his union to undertake a strike, Chavez recognized a growing restlessness and spirit for confrontation among the workers. He realized that to turn his back on a strike so close to home and so close to the workers he represented would be emotionally demoralizing. He knew his union was not ready for a strike but he also knew that, in these circumstances, he was not going to be responsible for breaking it. He decided to ask the membership to vote on whether to join the Filipinos and turn this small, infant protest into a big-time fight against the growers. He knew what their answer would be.

After Gilbert Padilla's introduction, Chavez, dressed in an old sport shirt and work pants, stepped up to speak to the large gathering, many of whom had never before seen or met him, although his name was fast becoming known throughout the migrant communities of central California. Short in stature, his voice halting and somewhat shaky, Chavez, nevertheless, rallied the men and woman to *La Causa*.

> You are here to discuss a matter which is of extreme importance to yourselves, your families and your community.... So let's get to the subject at hand. A hundred and fifty-five years ago, in the state of Guanajuato in Mexico, a padre proclaimed the struggle for liberty. He was killed, but ten years later Mexico won its independence.... We Mexicans here in the United States, as well as all other farm workers, are engaged in another struggle for the freedom and dignity which poverty denies us. But it must not be a violent struggle, even if violence is used against us. Violence can only hurt us and our cause. The law is for us as well as the ranchers. The strike was begun by the Filipinos, but it is not exclusively for them. Tonight we must decide if we are to join our fellow workers.[1]

Eliseo Medina, then an 18-year-old farmworker, later remembered attending the meeting at the church:

> Then they call a meeting for Our Lady of Guadalupe on September 16. Everybody's full of revolutionary fervor. So I go to the meeting. Even though I didn't like church much. It's packed. I'd never met Cesar Chavez.... He wasn't a great speaker, but he started talking and made a lot of sense. We deserved to be paid a fair wage. Because we're poor we shouldn't be taken advantage of. We had rights too in this country. We deserve more. The strike wouldn't be easy. The more he said how tough it would be the more people wanted to do it. By time the meeting ended ... that was it for me.[2]

Eliseo Medina was on board for *La Causa* and so was everyone else at the meeting. Here in this Catholic church, Chavez was leading something of a revival—not a religious movement, although it had the trappings and surroundings of religion, but a revival of the spirit. They shouted. They sang. They carried flags. They gloried in being part of the beginning of a movement. The editors of *El Malcriado* wrote of the phenomenon:

> What is a movement? It is when there are enough people with one idea so that their actions are together like the huge wave of water,

which nothing can stop. It is when a group of people begins to care enough so that they are willing to make sacrifices. The movement of the Negro began in the hot summer of Alabama ten years ago when a Negro woman refused to be pushed to the back of the bus. Thus began a gigantic wave of protest throughout the South. The Negro is willing to fight for what is his, an equal place under the sun. Sometime in the future they will say that in the hot summer of California in 1965 the movement of the farm workers began. It began with a small series of strikes. It started so slowly that at first it was only one man, then five, then one hundred. This is how a movement begins. This is why the Farm Workers Association is a movement more than a union.[3]

The NFWA voted unanimously to go forward with the strike that night at the church. The cry was now *"Viva la huelga!"* ("Long live the strike!"). Personally, Chavez remained cautious. The union had $100 in its bank account. But Chavez, by his decision to move forward, had put himself and his union not only in the forefront of an unprecedented effort to improve the lives of agricultural field workers but had also staked his own ground in the struggle for civil rights.

THE NATIONAL DRIVE FOR CIVIL RIGHTS

In 1954, when Chavez was in his first years with Fred Ross and the Community Service Organization, the U.S. Supreme Court issued a momentous decision. In *Brown v. Board of Education*, the Court struck down the doctrine of "separate but equal" that had stood as the law of the land since the turn of the century. That doctrine allowed governments to segregate black students from white students if they provided equal educational opportunities. In fact, many schools in the United States, especially in the South, had been separate but very unequal in their treatment of black students. In its decision, the Court declared that separating children solely on the classification of the color of their skin was unconstitutional. The decision paved the way for school integration and was the first major step in what would be a long fight for civil rights for black Americans.

As the civil rights struggle in these years turned on the fundamental issue of equal treatment and the policies of segregation, a black woman named Rosa Parks, a seamstress for the Montgomery Fair department store, crossed a significant dividing line and the civil rights movement never looked back. Active in the work of the National Association for the Advancement of Colored People (NAACP), Rosa Parks knew well the Montgomery, Alabama, law requiring blacks to surrender their seats on public buses if segregated white sections were full. Blacks had to pay fares at the front door and then enter the bus at the rear door to avoid contact with white passengers. She was also convinced that any challenge to the law should be done with nonviolence, dignity, and determination.

On December 1, 1955, she boarded the Cleveland Avenue bus and took a seat in the fifth row in front of the "Colored Section." The driver notified the police, who arrested Parks for violating city and state ordinances. Parks was released on $100 bond. Following Rosa Parks's arrest, several political activists in the city quickly gave the word to fellow workers to mimeograph thousands of leaflets calling for a boycott of the city buses on Monday, December 5, the day of the scheduled trial of Rosa Parks. They also asked a young minister and activist from Atlanta, Martin Luther King Jr., pastor of Dexter Baptist Church, to lead the boycott. Rosa Parks pleaded not guilty but was convicted and fined $14.

Rosa Parks's arrest and Martin Luther King's leadership of the Montgomery bus boycott were calls to action, catalysts that would drive the civil rights movement for many years. King would put to work the nonviolent activism that he had learned from the teachings of Gandhi.

National attention was now focused on Montgomery and the boycott. In December 1956 the U.S. Supreme Court declared Alabama's segregation laws unconstitutional and Montgomery buses were desegregated. The decision was another milestone in the civil rights movement and one of many of King's towering achievements.

From his vantage point in California, Cesar Chavez, like King a student of nonviolent protest and the teachings of Gandhi, began to absorb the tactics used in the protests and appreciate the ways in which the struggles of the Mexican Americans echoed the plight of black Americans.

The Supreme Court decision fueled the passion and determination of King and his followers. In 1957, they formed the Southern Christian Leadership Conference (SCLC). The bus desegregation success had proved that nonviolent direct action could succeed. Embodying the vision and philosophy of King, the SCLC fostered a mass movement based upon the Christian tenets of love and understanding.

Black students started "sit-ins" at lunch counters in the South. If they were not served, they would not leave. The sit-ins spread to various cities. Many of the students were jailed. But gradually they gained successes. King led marches in which protestors faced water hoses, jail cells, and beatings. Some were killed. But the movement spread.

In the spring of 1963, King led mass demonstrations in Birmingham. It was then that the name of Eugene "Bull" Connor, the chief of police, became closely linked with attack dogs and fire hoses, which he used on unarmed black protestors. Those dogs and those streams of water that knocked over scores of men, women, and children on the streets of Birmingham proved the efficacy of King's strategy of nonviolent confrontation. Despite the pain and injuries and overwhelming indignities suffered, the protestors prevailed. Their campaigns resulted in desegregated restrooms, drinking fountains, and lunch counters in Birmingham and an agreement by business leaders to hire and promote more black employees. Responding to the Birmingham protests, President John F. Kennedy submitted broad civil rights legislation to Congress, which eventually led to the passage of the Civil Rights Act of 1964, a year before Chavez decided to strike against California's grape growers.

On August 28, 1963, approximately a quarter of a million individuals gathered at the Lincoln Memorial in Washington, D.C. From all parts of the United States and abroad, they came to call for a redress of grievances against black Americans. They, along with millions of viewers of televisions across the world, heard King, many for the first time. They heard him deliver in thunderous and moving images his "I Have a Dream" speech, his vision of what the United States could be—a nation in which all of its citizens were measured by their character, not by the color of their skin.

King and other SCLC leaders were indefatigable in rallying town after town and community after community to accept their strategy of confronting government and business power with nonviolent methods; to take on the always discouraging odds for the cause of racial justice and civil rights; to put behind them the taunts and threats of the mobs, and to keep on working, and singing, and marching. From one town to another, from one set of circumstances to another, they challenged the power with their marches, boycotts, and sit-ins. They took on racism in an orderly, structured, and peaceful series of campaigns. In his mind, Cesar Chavez began to see as possible that the most lowly of America's workers, the men, women, and children in the fields, could also, with dynamic leadership, carry on their own fight for justice.

In March 1965, King organized a march from Selma, Alabama, to the state capitol of Birmingham to push for voting rights. On March 7, some 600 marchers headed east on U.S. Route 80. When they reached the Edmund Pettus Bridge six blocks away, state and local police attacked with Billy clubs and tear gas and drove them back into the city. The day became known as "Bloody Sunday." Two weeks later, with court protection and with the nation watching, about 3,200 marchers set for Montgomery, walking about 12 miles a day and sleeping in fields. The march reached Montgomery on March 25, now numbering 25,000 people.

On, August 6, 1965, President Lyndon Johnson signed the Voting Rights Act of 1965, providing federal protection for black citizens wishing to vote. Through the protests and marches, black Americans experienced a birth of feeling about their own value, a pride in their culture, and new hope for the future. And now, in a small Catholic church in Delano, California, a little over a month after President Johnson signed the Voting Rights Act, Chavez issued his own call to action, his own call for equal rights and social justice.

DOGGED, DETERMINED, AND NONVIOLENT

From the earliest days of the strike, Chavez preached to his troops the message of nonviolent confrontation. It worked in the civil rights movement; it would work, he believed, in the fields of California. "In the beginning," Chavez wrote later, "the staff people didn't thoroughly understand the whole idea of nonviolence, so I sent out the word to get young people who had been in the South and knew how to struggle non-violently. That's how we got our first volunteers—people from the Congress of Racial Equality and the Student Nonviolent Coordinating Committee who had been in the Civil Rights Movement. They were very good at teaching nonviolent tactics."[4]

Although some of his fellow strike leaders urged Chavez not to recruit extensively from outside the Delano area, he followed his own instinct to bring in the widest group of supporters he could, even though his enemies charged the movement with communist infiltration. They were, however, not communists, as FBI investigations would clearly discover over the years. They were students, civil rights workers, priests, ministers, rabbis, social workers, union leaders, and others who saw a chance to help a just cause. Chavez later said that the infusion of so many individuals of differing backgrounds, perspective, and experience added a wealth of ideas to the movement.

Chavez also began to coordinate strategy with the Agricultural Workers Organizing Committee (AWOC), the AFL-CIO-affiliated farmworkers' union, through its leader Al Green. The two men began to set strategy and coordinate activity.

Covering an area of more that 400 square miles, the strike force soon involved thousands of workers. For most of them, this was a first-time experience. Nevertheless, they learned quickly. Although they could not set up picket lines at all of the ranches at the same time, the strikers selectively forced down work at a number of the larger ranches and set in motion the inevitable next phase—the retaliation of the growers.

Led by DiGiorgio Fruit Corporation, Schenley Vineyards Corporation, and other major companies, the growers began to bring in scab labor to replace the union workers. Soon, the new workers, many of whom had no idea they had been brought in to replace striking workers, were being persuaded to put down their hoes and join the strike. Carrying signs flying the union's black eagle and calling for *Huelga*, the picketers, who at Chavez' insistence remained nonviolent, were surprisingly effective.

Progressively, the strikebreaking attempts became more and more ugly. Local police arrested workers attempting to enter some of the ranches. Ranch foremen, racing their pickup trucks up and down the strike lines, choked the picketers with dust. Some sprayed the picketers with sulfur and other chemicals and brandished shotguns. The foreman brought in dogs to intimidate the strikers. When the dust from the pickups was not enough, they began to run tractors by them to create even greater dust storms. They set up barricades of farm machinery so that the scab workers could not see the pickets. They fired buckshot through picket signs.

The Dispoto brothers, Charles and Bruno, well-known grape growers in the area, were especially notorious, daily walking alongside the picketers, calling them communists, trying to incite the strikers to violence. It did not work. Adhering to the nonviolent pledge they had all made to Chavez, they remained stoic amidst the insults, obscenities, and punches.

The determination of the strikers seemed to increase with the ferocity of methods used to put them down. Many of the scab laborers, upon seeing the treatment meted out to the strikers, decided to join them. Soon, the fruit fields of California were beginning to resemble scenes from the American south that had become so disturbing to television viewers throughout America.

When picketers were injured, they were cared for by fellow strikers. Their attackers went unpunished by local authorities. Indeed, the Delano Police Department and the Kern County Sheriff's Department began their own campaign of harassment. They photographed every striker on the picket lines. They recorded license plate numbers of everyone they could see who was involved with Chavez. They forced strikers to fill out cards asking for personal information and, with the help of the state Department of Motor Vehicles, compiled dossiers on the individuals. They even began to force strikers deep into the fields and away from roads so that their songs and shouts would go unheard. Nevertheless, despite the intimidation, the nonviolent protest continued and the picketers drew up more signs, chanted their strike cheers more loudly, and increased their numbers.

Even though Chavez and his lieutenants did not at first have a strike fund, the national publicity garnered through the print and television media and the intense fundraising activity that the leaders began to employ soon after the strike began started to pay off. College students from California universities and even from out of state began to show up at the work sites to volunteer. Checks began arriving from individuals across the country who were appalled at the treatment of the strikers and who had begun to learn more about the cause for which the strikers were fighting. Large unions like the United Auto Workers also began to lend financial support. Civil rights, church, and fraternal groups helped with both food and money. In newspapers and on radio and television, Americans now learned of the unfolding events. Chavez was especially diligent in reporting every instance of violence to the press.

On Friday evenings Chavez began to hold two-hour meetings. Meant to bolster the spirit and camaraderie of the strikers, the weekly gatherings included songs, skits, testimonials from families and friends of the strikers, and presentations by guests from religious, social, and labor organizations. They also included performances by El Teatro Campesino (The Farmworkers' Theater).

Founded and directed by aspiring playwright and actor Luis Valdez, El Teatro Campesino, combining Mexican folk theater, comedy, and mime, offered comic reflections on laborers, bosses, and others in the world of the farmworker. The actors themselves were campesinos (farmworkers). The company created short skits that they performed on the Friday night gatherings as well as on flatbed trucks at the strike sites. They later toured towns and cities to raise money for the union.

A typical skit would include the "*Huelguista*" (striker), the "*Patroncita*" (grower), the "*Contratista*" (farm labor contractor), and the "*Esquirol*" (scab or strikebreaker). The theater performances varied from week to week depending on the specific progress or setbacks experienced by the strikers.

In addition to a stream of attacks and ridicule against the growers and their hired strikebreakers, the performances consistently used a translation from the writer Jack London in describing a scab. "After God finished the rattlesnake, the toad, and the vampire," the translation went, "he had some awful substance left with which he made a strikebreaker. A strikebreaker is a two-legged animal with a corkscrew soul, a waterlogged brain, and a combination backbone made of jelly and glue. Where others had hearts, he carried a tumor of rotten principles."[5]

Luis Valdez, who went on to an extraordinary career in the theater, had grown up in Delano as a teenager and had known Chavez well. He returned to his old friend, he recalled later,

> to go back to my roots, to go back among the campesinos, and that's the choice that I took. I went back, I was a social activist, a child of the '60s, so in that sense I wanted to change the world. I decided to go back to Delano and try to change this valley that treated Mexicans the way the south treated African Americans. We were fighting for our civil rights, for our humanity, and it seemed to me that using the arts, using humor, using masks, using theatre, was the way to do it.[6]

Several times a week "Huelga Priests" held masses for the workers. People began to talk about Mexican history and the relationship of this strike to other battles of the poor and dispossessed. Slogans appeared on the sides of buildings and fences. Strikers waved banners of the Virgin of Guadalupe, the patron saint of Mexico, and carried both the Mexican and U.S. flags.

All of this helped establish a strong sense of solidarity and cultural identity among the group and discouraged other workers who heard the plays and the other Friday evening activities from staying with the growers. For many of the workers it was all exhilarating, if dangerous, and something quite out of the ordinary in the lives of farm laborers, like a drink of fine wine after years of tainted water.

By late October, the counterstrike forces began to arrest picketers on the charge of disturbing the peace. One picketer, Reverend David Havens of the California Migrant Ministry, was hurried off to jail when he stood on the back of a flatbed truck and recited Jack London's piece on strikebreakers. A few days later, the sheriff's department took the campaign to new heights of nonsense when it declared that the picketers were forbidden to use the word *Huelga*. When Chavez learned of this prohibition, he welcomed the opportunity to capitalize. He notified the press that they should be on hand for some breaking news.

With newspaper and television camera crews at work and press writers taking down notes, Helen Chavez, accompanied by 13 farmworkers and several clergymen from the San Francisco area, met outside the W.B. Camp Ranch near Delano. Taking up positions across from a harvest crew, the team began shouting as loudly as possible. *"Huelga! Huelga! Huelga! Huelga!"*—the forbidden word thundered incessantly.

The sheriff and his men dutifully arrested 44 pickets and escorted them to the Bakersfield jail. With bail at $276 each, the men and women of the unlawful assembly prepared to spend three days in jail.

For Chavez, the incident was a political godsend. The union leader, in speeches to students at the University of California, Stanford University, and Mills College, told of the egregious outrage to free speech and they responded. They sent telegrams to Delano; they donated to the cause. Chavez returned with nearly $7,000. Soon, a contingent of 350 protestors gathered in front of the county courthouse, singing protest songs. Helen was freed along with the others and the sheriff's order rescinded.

After absorbing the first round of volleys from the growers, Chavez decided to raise the level of the protest. In early December 1965, he decided to call a boycott of Schenley Vineyards. Recruiting additional volunteers from churches, community organizations, labor organizations, and universities, the union set up boycott centers in the cities. Signs appeared urging the public to "Help Farmworkers—Do Not Buy Grapes." The protest had thus moved from the fields to the urban areas. It also attracted additional national attention.

In December, Walter Reuther, head of the United Auto Workers, visited Chavez in support of the strike and boycott. Armed with some money and heartfelt enthusiasm, Reuther joined the workers on a march through Delano to union headquarters. There, he gave an impassioned speech and later held a press conference heavily attended by the national press.

It quickly became clear that Chavez was no ordinary leader and this was no ordinary strike. This was more than a typical fight for wages and working conditions; Chavez had focused the movement on the ethnic identity of Mexican Americans and a on quest for justice rooted in Catholic social teaching.

Appropriately, Luis Valdez, the director of El Teatro Campesino, helped the union create a cultural center for farmworkers and their families in Delano, where, through art, music, dance, and the theater, they could learn about Mexican heritage. Valdez considered Chavez's work as a quest to obtain for Mexican American workers simple human dignity. The strikers' informal anthem became "*De Colores*," a Spanish religious hymn.

De colores, de colores se visten los campos en la primavera.
De colores, de colores son los pajaritos que vienen deafuera.
De colores, de colores es el arco iris que vemos lucir.
Y por eso los grandes amores de muchos colores me gustan a mi,
Y por eso los grandes amores de muchos colores me gustan a mi.

(In colors, in colors the fields in the spring dress up.
In colors, in colors the little birds come from far off.
In colors, in colors the rainbow we see glistening,
And that's why those big many-colored loves are what I like,
And that's why those big many-colored loves are what I like.)[7]

Later, William Kircher, an AFL-CIO organizer with the farmworkers,
described the farmworkers' march as "New. Radical. Different. A crew of
people walking along the highway carrying the banner of Our Lady, calling meetings at night which attracted farm workers out of the fields and
towns, opening with 'De Colores,' ... maybe a prayer. The whole thing
had a strong cultural, religious thing, it was organizing people."[8]

MARCHING TO SACRAMENTO

Through the winter months into 1966, Chavez gathered supporters
to explore ways to maintain the fervor and commitment of the strikers.
In February, at a meeting near Santa Barbara, the union leader and his
advisors, after discussing a number of strategic possibilities, decided to adopt
another tactic that had been successful in the civil rights movement—
a long march. It would cover a route from Delano to the state capitol
of Sacramento, through such towns as Madera, Fresno, Modesto, and
Stockton. For Chavez, however, the march would emphasize the religious
spirit behind the union movement.

A minister who joined the march said, "I'm here because this is a
movement by the poor people themselves to improve their position, and
where the poor people are, Christ should be and is."[9]

Union organizer Marshall Ganz recorded in his diary a revealing sug-
gestion made at the meeting by Chavez: "... then Chavez asked, why
should it be a 'march' at all? It will be Lent soon, a time for reflection,
for penance, for asking forgiveness. Perhaps ours should be a pilgrimage, a
'peregrinacion,' which could arrive at Sacramento on Easter Sunday."[10]

In an attempt to connect even further the union movement with the
history and culture of Mexico, Luis Valdez suggested that they write a
"Plan de Delano" to be read in each town through which they marched.
The statement would follow in the tradition of a leader of the Mexican
Revolution, Emiliano Zapata, who fought for the rights of native peoples
against powerful landowners. In 1911, Zapata put forward his "Plan de
Alaya," a rallying statement for the underclasses. Chavez asked Valdez
to compose such a document for the farmworkers. It became yet another
symbol around which the strikers rallied.

"This is the beginning of a social movement in fact and not in pro-
nouncements," the document read. "We seek our basic, God-given rights
as human beings. Because we have suffered—and are not afraid to suffer
in order to survive, we are ready to give up everything, even our lives, in
our fight for social justice. We shall do it without violence because that is
our destiny." The document talked of a pilgrimage to seek an end to the
suffering of farmworkers; of their determination to be heard; and of their
resolve to follow their God. It promised unity with people of all faiths and
races; inclusion of all races and workers across the land; and a revolution
for "bread and justice."[11]

On the morning of March 17, 1966, Chavez and about 100 individuals
gathered in Delano to begin the march. Somewhat disorganized but enthusiastic they set off through the town and onto Highway 99, followed by
members of the press, several FBI agents, and other onlookers. Soon, they
began to pass some of the vineyards in which they had worked and against
which they had organized pickets six months earlier. They carried banners,
portraits of the Virgin of Guadalupe, and union flags. Some carried large
crosses. Some wore Veterans of Foreign Wars hats. Luis Valdez carried "The
Plan of Delano" to be read at each stop and signed by local workers.

As the marchers began to reach small towns, local workers and their
families, yelling and shouting, would run toward them and swell their
numbers. They cooked hamburgers, tortillas, and beans and rice to feed
those in the protest. Covering about 15 miles a day, some of those who had
started the journey in Delano began to suffer blistered feet. Chavez was
one of those. FBI informants kept their Washington superiors informed
of the progress. By the time they had reached Stockton, one of the informants reported, the march had grown to approximately 1,500, many of
whom were provided lodging by locals in the towns through which they
passed. As the marchers walked through the towns they lit candles.

As it progressed through the San Joaquin Valley toward Sacramento,
the march drew increasing national publicity, with many reporters comparing it to the Selma to Montgomery civil rights march a year earlier.
On April 3 in Chicago, several Hispanic organizations used the occasion of their annual sidewalk parade in connection with Holy Week to
demonstrate their solidarity with the 300-mile pilgrimage in California.
Beginning at St. Francis Assisi Church in Chicago's near west side
Mexican American and Puerto Rican neighborhoods, marchers carried
placards reading *Huelga* and sang anthems as they trooped down the
streets to St. Pius Church.

As Catholic and Episcopal bishops voiced support for the strike and
as rabbis appeared along the route to share Passover with the marchers,

it was clear that Chavez, now limping badly on his swollen feet and using a cane, had succeeded in framing the march in religious as well as cultural terms. He had also succeeded in casting the strike, not as a labor action or a left-wing political maneuver, but as a fight for justice.

At each stop Valdez pulled out his copy of "The Plan of Delano" and read it aloud:

WE SHALL OVERCOME. Across the San Joaquin Valley, across California, across the entire Southwest of the United States, wherever there are Mexican people, wherever there are farm workers, our movement is spreading like flames across [a] dry plain. Our PILGRIMAGE is the MATCH that will light our cause for all farm workers to see what is happening here, so that they may do as we have done. The time has come for the liberation of the poor farm worker. History is on our side. MAY THE STRIKE GO ON! VIVA LA CAUSA![12]

On April 3, a week before the marchers were due to reach Sacramento, Chavez received a call from a representative of Schenley Vineyards. Already damaged by the publicity garnered by Chavez and hurt economically by the strike and boycott, the company had decided to cut its losses. They decided to enter into negotiations with Chavez for a union contract. Anxious to settle before the marchers reached Sacramento and the inevitable landslide of publicity that the event would produce, the company signed a preliminary agreement. Dolores Huerta was charged with drawing up a full contract that would be finalized within 90 days.

The company agreed to recognize formally the National Farm Workers Association. This was the first time in U.S. history that a grassroots, farm-labor union had achieved recognition by a corporation. Schenley agreed to a substantial increase of wages and to an improvement of working conditions.

On Saturday afternoon, the marchers rested on the grounds of Our Lady of Grace School on a hill looking across the Sacramento River to the capital city and held a rally that evening. Roberto Roman, a farm-worker who had carried a wooden cross draped in black cloth for the entire 300 miles from Delano, stayed up most of the night redraping it in white and covering it with flowers.

The next morning, Easter 1966, Roman joined Chavez and 50 other *originales* who had walked the entire distance. Led by several supporters on horseback carrying the union flag and many others wearing sombreros, they marched triumphantly across the bridge, down the mall, and up the capitol steps to thunderous cheers.

NOTES

1. John Gregory Dunne, *Delano: The Story of the California Grape Strike* (New York: Farrar, Straus and Giroux, 1967), 77–80.

2. Marshall Ganz, "The Power of Story in Social Movements," Harvard University, ksghome.harvard.edu/~mganz/MG%20POWER%20OF%20STORY.pdf.

3. Ibid.

4. Jacques Levy, *Cesar Chavez: Autobiography of La Causa*, http://chavez. cde.ca.gov/ModelCurriculum/Teachers/Lessons/Resources/Documents/Chavez_Biography_by_Levy.PDF.

5. Robbie Stockman, "A Multifaceted Experience in El Teatro Campesino," http://people.ucsc.edu/~dramadon/Campesino_paper.htm.

6. "Texas Touring Arts Conference, 2002: Luis Valdez Keynote," http://www. arts.state.tx.us/ttac/valdez.asp.

7. Michael Richmond, "The Music of Labor: From Movement to Culture," *Legal Studies Forum* (1999), http://tarlton.law.utexas.edu/lpop/etext/lsf/richm23.htm.

8. Ed Schwartz, "Cesar Chavez: Leader as Organizer, http://www.iscv.org/Opportunity/CesarChavez/cesarchavez.html.

9. Dick Meister, "'La Huelga' Becomes 'La Causa,'" *New York Times Magazine* (17 November 1968), 92.

10. "Chavez Banner," *History Detectives,* http://pbs.org/opb/historydetectives/pdf/209_banner.pdf.

11. "The Plan of Delano," http://www.sfsu.edu/~cecipp/cesar_chavez/delanoeng.htm.

12. "The Plan of Delano."

A migrant Mexican worker and his children, circa 1930s/1940s. Reproduced courtesy of the Library of Congress.

Cesar Chavez and wife, Helen, during a strike in Delano, California, 1966. Reproduced courtesy of the Library of Congress.

Cahavez in 1966—this is the year The United Farm Workers Organizing Committee (later to become the United Farm Workers of America, AFL-CIO) is formed under the direction of Chavez. Reproduced courtesy of the Library of Congress.

Stoop labor—melon picker in California field. Reproduced courtesy of the
Library of Congress.

Chavez leading a boycott on bananas. Reproduced courtesy of the Library of Congress.

Chavez gathering supporters. Reproduced courtesy of the U.S. National Archives.

Chapter 6

IN THE TUMULT

BOYCOTT

In the spring of 1966, Chavez's union stayed on the attack, launching a boycott against DiGiorgio Fruit Corporation, a giant grape growing enterprise near Bakersfield, California, whose interests included TreeSweet juices and S&W Fine Foods. Since its founding, DiGiorgio had gained a reputation for taking ruthless action to keep union organizers far from its workers.

Faced with the determined leadership of Chavez, the company had by early 1967 agreed to hold an election among its workers to determine whether they wanted to be represented by the union. The gesture was not what it seemed on the surface. DiGiorgio had a new strategy in place to combat the growing power of the union headed by Chavez. They decided to turn to the giant International Brotherhood of Teamsters union, whose leadership was anxious to incorporate the farmworkers under its own enormous control. In order to gain a foothold in this new labor area, the Teamsters, DiGiorgio realized, would offer much more favorable contract terms than the fledgling but spirited National Farm Workers Association (NFWA), led by Chavez. DiGiorgio invited the Teamsters to organize company workers with no job security, seniority rights, or hiring hall. The Teamsters agreed.

In the summer, the company held an election in which the farmworkers apparently chose to be represented by the Teamsters. After reports of numerous cases of voter irregularity, an investigation by the California state government proved that the election had been rigged. The company agreed to a new election to be held on August 30, 1967.

A few weeks before the election, Chavez employed a counter-strategy. He agreed to merge the NFWA with the Agricultural Workers Organizing Committee (AWOC), with whom he had been working in the Delano strike. Together, they would form the United Farm Workers Organizing Committee (UFWOC) and affiliate with the AFL-CIO, the national labor federation. On August 22, the two organizations officially united. Chavez and his union would now receive organizing funds from the AFL-CIO, as well as strike support from other affiliated unions consisting of food, cash, and office equipment.

In the ensuring election, the workers at DiGiorgio overwhelming voted to support UFWOC, headed by Chavez. Soon afterward, the company agreed to sign a three-year contract. In addition to providing the workers greater wages and benefits, including a yearly one-week vacation, the agreement granted a "hiring hall" provision stipulating that DiGiorgio must give the union 72 hours to produce workers before it could hire outside workers.

George Meany, president of the AFL-CIO, telegrammed Chavez after DiGiorgio signed the contract. "It should be clear notice to growers everywhere," he told Chavez, "that the AFL-CIO will not rest until all farm workers—until now the most exploited workers in the United States—have the same opportunity to better their lives as other workers have."[1]

Chavez had gained another victory. The effort by the Teamsters and DiGiorgio to break up Chavez's union was temporarily stalled. Nevertheless, the Teamsters' leadership remained undeterred and would continue to fight to undermine the UFWOC. He knew that he was fighting not only the growers but also a rival union.

By 1967, the farmworkers' union numbered about 8,000 members. Chavez, as unlikely and unusual a union leader as the nation had ever seen, remained cautious yet exuberant in his early successes. The membership of the union had spread outside the boundaries of California and so had its influence.

Chavez now turned his sights on the Giumarra Vineyards Corporation, the largest producer of table grapes in the United States. "Giumarra is one of the biggest growers," Dolores Huerta told a newspaper reporter, "and if we can crack Giumarra we can crack them all."[2] Irked by the targeting of his company, a Giumarra official dismissed the farmworkers' union as "socialist-civil rights movement" aided by "do-gooder elements, beatniks and socialistic-type groups."[3]

Another grower, frustrated by the appeal of Chavez and his growing movement, said, "Chavez's secret is that he has the utter loyalty of the Mexican workers. His appeal is primarily racial—and to some extent religious. They're not a trade union, they're a racial and religious organization."[4]

Chavez never backed away from these contentions. Indeed, on occasion the protestors held "pray ins" across from the entrances to ranches. Chavez even asked his brother Richard to build a portable, wooden altar to fit in the back of his station wagon, where picketers could find religious comfort during the long days. Needless to say, such demonstrations frustrated company owners and their strikebreaking tactics. It was one thing to fight the usual labor battles; it was another to take on the kind of spiritual and cultural assault being waged by Chavez.

This strike, Chavez believed, would represent much more than merely labor conditions in the fields of California. As it gained momentum, Mexican Americans would rally to La Causa because for them it symbolized their own cultural and racial struggle in American society. This battle represented their aspirations for a better life. For many Mexican Americans across the country, at the time numbering approximately five million, the sight of the workers raising the black Aztec eagle on a red field and the images of the Virgin of Guadalupe struck a deep chord. Richard Chavez later wrote, "What Cesar wanted to reform was the way he was treated as a man."[5]

In the early days of the antislavery movement in the United States, the reformers used the phrase "Am I Not a Man and a Brother?" Now, in the 1960s, Chavez was asking that same basic question on behalf of his fellow Mexican American workers. Their fight and his was for respect and dignity.

He was doing it from his tiny two-bedroom house in Delano where, for a number of years, his wife and eight children found a way to share the small amount of space. The family was living on $10 a week from the union and on food from a communal kitchen in the nearby union headquarters. As the union began completely to dominate his time and energy, Chavez had almost given up even casual socializing. He no longer smoked or drank alcohol. He liked Chinese food and matzos along with traditional Mexican food and low-calorie sodas. Later, as he reached middle age, he would at times try a vegetarian diet and experiment with yoga.

As the days of the strike grew longer, Chavez told a reporter that it seemed as if he could not remember a time when they were not on strike. "Either the union will be destroyed," he said, "or they will sign a contract. There's no other alternative."[6]

In response to the boycott, Giumarra turned to other grape growers for support and they responded. The growers agreed to allow Giumarra to use their own labels for Giumarra's grapes. Thus, even if the public refused to buy the Giumarra brand, the company would be relatively unhurt by the boycott.

Undeterred, Chavez upped the stakes. If the other growers in California wanted to join Giumarra, then those companies would also be the targets of a boycott. Chavez decided to initiate a nationwide boycott of all table grapes from California.

Soon, across the nation, thousands of demonstrators picketed and marched asking the public not to purchase table grapes from California vineyards. Supermarket chains from the east coast to the west reacted in various ways. Some began purchasing grapes from Israel or Africa and refused to buy California grapes. Others decided to leave the choice to the purchaser and carried California grapes.

By the end of 1967, UFWOC leaders had carried on demonstrations and boycott activities in 34 cities across the country and the protests spread to Britain and Scandinavia. By 1968 nationwide grape sales had declined by 12 per cent. Chavez saw definite progress; however, he also saw danger ahead.

RAGE IN THE CITIES

As Chavez's boycott increased its intensity nationwide, the American civil rights movement was taking a more dangerous turn. As the movement directly challenged the existing economic and political power structures, as it demonstrated that reformers could indeed make a difference in the lives of ordinary minority citizens, it inevitably raised expectations and intensified pressures for immediate change. Thousands of black Americans who had been living their lives resigned to the racial caste system that deprived them of basic rights and opportunities now saw the chance for something better. But, as increasingly strident demands for change were met with fierce resistance and racial animosity, the delicate stability in many urban centers of America blew apart.

In August 1965 the Los Angeles neighborhood of Watts exploded in rioting after a traffic incident. The hostility between the black neighborhood and the Los Angeles police, inflamed throughout the summer, erupted into such chaos and violence that more than 30 people were killed, almost all of them black. More than 3,500 people were arrested, many for looting stores and setting fire to buildings and automobiles. The clash was of such a magnitude that the National Guard was called out to restore order.

In the summer of 1967, many of Martin Luther King Jr.'s deepest worries about the growing violence were realized. America's ghettos were aflame.

Even as victories had mounted in the civil rights campaign against segregation and disfranchisement and had raised hopes in the black communities around the country for progress toward racial equality, the attempts to force economic rights in the north met with a fiery resistance that even King had not foreseen. The sight of rioting black youths in the inner cities fighting with police became a frightening if not uncommon spectacle on American television news. More than 75 cities witnessed especially brutal confrontations in 1967 alone.

In Newark, New Jersey, 26 blacks lost their lives amid the carnage and in Detroit, Michigan, riots lasted a full week with the city's black areas ablaze and enveloped by billowing black clouds of smoke. More than 40 individuals lost their lives in the Detroit riots. King condemned the violence but his harshest criticism was for the social conditions that he believed led to the violence. When King had visited Watts in 1965 after the riots, he said that officials in the city should have anticipated them as the unemployment rate in Watts had soared and its population density had become the highest in the nation. America's war with itself over racial equality and equal rights, King knew, would be a long one.

King himself was now under attack by aggressive black leaders who demanded that the movement turn from nonviolence. They called for "Black Power" and urged all blacks not to turn their backs on the physical assaults they continually endured but to resist forcefully. Even with the progress that King had already achieved, it was becoming increasingly difficult for him to control an explosive social climate of hatred and fear that threatened to unravel many of the civil rights advances already gained.

Cesar Chavez watched the national developments with increasing anxiety. Within his own union membership there were similar rustlings of discontent. The personal pressures on the strikers, many of who were nearly impoverished and the target of increasing harassment and physical abuse, were enormous. They found it increasingly difficult to stand by their pledge to Chavez to remain nonviolent. When one of the strikers was nearly killed by a car that ran through a picket line near Delano, a group of protestors managed to surround the driver of the car. Fortunately, Chavez was nearby and escorted the man to the company headquarters. Even though some of the strikers were angry at Chavez for intervening, some of the men and women who were on the scene that day said that he had probably saved the driver's life.

Disturbing news reached Chavez from other areas. Some of the strikers had blown up irrigation pumps, flattened tires, and roughed up a number of individuals they suspected of being company spies. Chavez even had to confiscate guns from a few of the strikers and send others home who were increasingly combative.

In a book of notes that Chavez wrote during this period, he said, "It's very tough. I don't know if I can continue." Nevertheless, in a testament to the influence and support that Helen gave to Chavez, a note from a few days later said, "I spoke to Helen. I'm ready to go."[7]

Chavez was determined that the movement would not be swallowed up in destructive violence. He said, "By and large, people oppose violence. So when government or growers use violence against us, we strategize around it. We can respond nonviolently, because that swings people to our side, and that gives us our strength. First, of course, the workers have to understand nonviolence. Gandhi once said he'd rather have a man be violent than be a coward.... If he's a coward, then what good is he for anyone."[8]

REASSERTING NONVIOLENCE: THE FAST

By early February 1968, Chavez's concern about increasing attitudes of violence in the ranks of his own protestors reached, for him, a critical point. Later, he recalled: "There was demoralization in the ranks, people becoming desperate, more and more talk about violence. People meant it, even when they talked to me ... I thought that I had to ... do something that would force them and me to deal with the whole question of violence and ourselves[.] We had to stop long enough to take account of what we were doing."[9]

For a student of Gandhi, the great Indian independence hero whose large portrait hung in Chavez's office, along with that of Martin Luther King Jr., the course Chavez chose in response to the increasing threat of violence in the ranks was not totally surprising. He decided to fast. It was what Gandhi had taught; it was what Gandhi himself had practiced. On February 14, Chavez stopped eating. At first, he told only a few of his closest friends. After a few days, the word spread quickly.

In many ways the fast was a logical extension of his fight for social change. It emphasized perfectly the approach of his movement—nonviolent, spiritual, a willingness to sacrifice for the greater good. Most of his fellow lieutenants, although very worried about the health of their leader, saw the extreme sacrificial gesture, religious in nature, as a way to rededicate the cause to nonviolence. He said, "If the strike means the blood of one grower or one grower's son, or one worker or one worker's son, then it isn't worth it."[10]

At the same time, Chavez was not unaware that the action of fasting, so unusual in American social and political life, would attract an extraordinary amount of publicity for the movement. He welcomed the visitors, the questions, and the attention.

After four days, he called a meeting of the strikers. When the civil rights movement had turned violent, he told his supporters, it was the blacks who suffered. It was they who lost their lives and their property and the support of the larger American community. Likewise, if the farm-workers' movement turned to violence, he said, it would be the poor who would suffer. This fast, he declared, was a call to recommit. He implored them not to lose faith or patience. He would continue to fast until he felt that the supporters of the movement as well as the American public fully understood what the fight was all about.

He had no plan to refuse food for any specific length of time. Increasingly worried about his ebbing strength, Helen frequently argued that everything that they were working for would be imperiled if he lost his health and even his life. Some of his close friends were angered by his actions; others understood. A few left the strike, convinced that Chavez was either undertaking a bad publicity stunt or that he had lost his mind and had delusions of sainthood. Many of the growers and other opponents saw the fast as nothing more than a theatrical stunt.

As the fast continued, Chavez received Communion every day. He asked that a daily mass be held at the union headquarters where he stayed. During the fast, Chavez again emphasized the importance of the religious connection to the movement. He said,

> When poor people get involved in a long conflict, such as a strike, or a civil rights drive, and the pressure increases each day, there is a deep need for spiritual advice. Without it we see families crumble, leadership weaken, and workers grow tired.... It is not just our right to appeal to the Church to use its power effectively for the poor, it is our duty to do so. It should be as natural as appealing to government ... and we do that often enough.[11]

During the fast, Martin Luther King, while preparing to lead a massive march on Washington later in the spring on behalf of the nation's poor, sent the following telegram in support:

> I am deeply moved by your courage in fasting as your personal sacri-fice for justice through nonviolence. Your past and present commit-ment is eloquent testimony to the constructive power of nonviolent action and the destructive impotence of violent reprisal. You stand today as a living example of the Gandhian tradition with its great

force for social progress and its healing spiritual powers. My colleagues and I commend you for your bravery, salute you for your indefatigable work against poverty and injustice, and pray for your health and your continuing service as one of the outstanding men of America. The plight of your people and ours is so grave that we all desperately need the inspiring example and effective leadership you have given.[12]

A number of individuals near to Chavez decided to show support by going on their own fasts. Dolores Huerta, Marshall Ganz, and Chavez's brother Richard all went without food for a number of days.

So did a number of individuals in other cities. One of them was Juanita Herrera, a long-time farmworker who had labored in the fields of New Mexico, Colorado, and California since the age of 12. Herrera, by now married and a mother of four, had eagerly followed La Causa from the moment she heard of Cesar Chavez. Along with nine others, she camped out on the lawn next to the Basilica of the Immaculate Conception in downtown Denver, Colorado. They fasted for 10 days, consuming only water, coffee, and tea.

There was no small irony, members of Chavez's team began to realize, that the fast had turned out to be one of the most dramatic organizing tools the new union had ever employed. Across the country, people from various backgrounds began to voice support for the union and its strike. The press flocked to Delano. Money arrived. All of this occurred when its leader was completely immobilized.

Many admirers began to bring religious icons to Chavez. He saw many of the visitors personally and some of the encounters were quite emotional. There were priests wearing vestments made from the cloth of farmworker flags; there people sleeping in the yard outside holding prayer rallies, drinking hot chocolate, and singing. Clearly, many individuals now held Chavez in an unusual degree of reverence and awe. Most of them were concerned that he might die.

Senator Robert F. Kennedy, who would announce his candidacy for president the following month, sent a telegram, in late February 1968, to Chavez, asking him to consider the consequences to the movement if he should not survive. Senator Kennedy was a strong supporter of both the civil rights movement and of the farm labor strike. He had worked to help poverty-stricken people in urban ghettos, Appalachia, the Mississippi Delta, and migrant workers' camps. Chavez, while working for the Community Service Organization, had first met Kennedy during a voter registration drive in 1959. They met again in 1966, three years after Robert Kennedy had lost his brother, President John F. Kennedy, to an assassin. Kennedy endorsed the farm labor struggle. He saw in their effort a clear link to other problems plaguing America—racism, poverty, and urban blight. They came to admire each other greatly.

For 21 days Chavez fasted. By the time he had lost 35 pounds and had grown progressively weaker, his doctor began to fear for his life. Chavez gave in to the entreaties of his friends and relatives and finally agreed to end the fast on March 10, 1968.

He did it with a celebration. A crowd of several thousand watched as Chavez, seated with his wife and mother, broke bread with Senator Kennedy, who had flown in for the event from a political dinner in Des Moines, Iowa. As Kennedy walked toward Chavez, to chants of "Bobby, Bobby, Bobby," hundreds of farmworkers crowded around him, trying to shake his hand or get in a word. Dolores Huerta remembered it as "the most wild moment in my life. All these farm workers really loved Bobby. They called him brother and saw him as more saint than politician."[13]

One of the journalists at the event said that Kennedy was almost engulfed. "It was hard to keep his feet on the ground as the crowd pushed hard," Ronald Taylor later recalled. Kennedy reached over our arms, smiling, touching, shaking hands."[14]

At an open-air mass, several priests and nuns distributed bread to the crowd. Chavez later remembered one particularly humorous moment during all the swirl of activity. After seeing Kennedy give Chavez a piece of bread, a cameraman who had lost a chance for good photograph asked Kennedy to give Chavez another piece. The photos of the event circulated around the world.

Addressing the crowd, Senator Kennedy said, "The world must know that the migrant farm worker, the Mexican-American, is coming into his own right." The victory would be theirs, Kennedy said, but they must do it with nonviolent means.[15]

Chavez was too weak even to stand up on March 10. Nevertheless, he had prepared some remarks about the purposes for which La Causa stood. They read in part:

Our lives are really all that belong to us. Only by giving our lives do we find light. I am convinced that the truest act of courage, the strongest act of manliness is to sacrifice ourselves for others in a totally non-violent struggle for justice. To be a man is to suffer for others. God help us be men.[16]

Max Kennedy, a son of Robert Kennedy, later said that when he looked back at the images of that day, "of my father and Cesar Chavez, two

American citizens sitting beside one another, breaking bread, extending themselves toward one another and to us, I think about what a wonderful country this is and how proud we should all be that this is the kind of country where two people like this can become brothers."[17]

Shortly after the fast, Kennedy made official his decision to run for president. Chavez responded by committing his union to campaign for Kennedy in the California primary race. In the midst of the continuing grape boycott, Chavez would help in a voter registration drive for Kennedy among Mexican Americans.

LOST BROTHERS

Less than three weeks after Chavez ended his fast, on the evening of April 3, 1968, Martin Luther King Jr. was in Memphis, Tennessee. In the middle of planning for a major march on Washington on behalf of the poor, he had stopped off in Memphis to support striking city sanitation workers. Delivering a speech at the Mason Temple, King talked about how far those people surrounding him had together come in the civil rights movement, how overwhelming had been the struggle, and how daunting remained the challenges ahead. He talked about a recent incident in which a troubled black woman had knifed him and that the knife had come perilously close to his aorta. He talked about the uncertainty of his own future and about recent threats on his own life. He told them to hold together for the cause of social equality, no matter what happened.

And then, in a remarkably prescient moment, he looked forward to difficult days ahead:

> But it doesn't matter with me now. Because I've been to the mountaintop. And I don't mind. Like anybody, I would like to live a long life. Longevity has its place. But I'm not concerned about that now. I just want to do God's will. And He's allowed me to go up to the mountain. And I've looked over. And I've seen the promised land. I may not get there with you. But I want you to know tonight, that we, as a people, will get to the promised land. And I'm happy, tonight. I'm not worried about anything. I'm not fearing any man. Mine eyes have seen the glory of the coming of the Lord.[18]

Early the following morning, April 4, King prepared to leave the Lorraine Motel to meet with march organizers. As he stepped out from his room on the second floor, he had only an instant more to live. When an assassin's rifle bullet ended his life that day in Memphis, he was 39 years old.

Chavez was stunned and profoundly saddened by King's assassination. The civil rights leader was not only a heroic figure to many Americans; he was also, in Chavez's mind, a great teacher. Chavez said, "Dr. King's dedication to the rights of the workers who are so often exploited by the forces of greed has profoundly touched my life and guided my struggle. Just as Dr. King was a disciple of Ghandi and Christ, we must now be Dr. King's disciples ... Dr. King challenged us to work for a greater humanity. I only hope that we are worthy of his challenge."[19]

In the wake of King's assassination, the work of Chavez and *La Causa* continued apace. For two months, Chavez's union troops eagerly honored their pledge to help Senator Kennedy in his bid for the White House. Throughout Chicano barrios in the major cities and in the harvesting areas of California, volunteers answered Chavez's call to help the Kennedy campaign. They canvassed door to door encouraging residents to register and vote. They helped bring out a large outpouring of Mexican American votes for the Senator on California's primary election day, June 4, 1968.

At the Ambassador Hotel in Los Angeles, Chavez, Dolores Huerta, and other friends of the farmworkers' union celebrated Kennedy's victory in the California primary election for the presidential nomination along with thousands of supporters in the hotel ballroom. Huerta was among many of Kennedy's friends and supporters on stage. Chavez waited in a private room of the hotel with a mariachi band that eagerly waited to play in the senator's honor.

After Kennedy completed his victory speech to a tumultuous ovation, he stayed for a while thanking personally many of those who had helped in his campaign, including Huerta. Along with several associates, Kennedy then walked off the stage, heading from the ballroom through the kitchen. They walked into pandemonium. A lone gunman named Sirhan Sirhan fired several shots, hitting Kennedy, who fell, gravely wounded, and several others. Kennedy died the following day.

Paul Schrade, a friend both of Senator Kennedy and Chavez, was one of those wounded that night. He later said of the two: "They cared. They believed. They acted. Theirs were hechos de amor, deeds of love. Robert often said, 'We can do better.' Cesar often said, '¡Si Se Puede!' We must continue to say, 'We can do better' and '¡Si Se Puede!' "[20] Chavez and the farmworkers' union had lost two towering and inspirational supporters. Devastated by the two assassinations within the space of two months, they would, nevertheless, carry on the fight.

In 1970, when Chavez was jailed for defying a court injunction against boycotting, he had a number of prominent visitors. They included Coretta

Scott King, widow of Martin Luther King Jr., and Ethel Kennedy, widow of Robert F. Kennedy. It was, Chavez thought, like a gathering of family.

AN EXPANDING BOYCOTT

In the summer of 1968, Douglas Foster was a member of a group of junior high school kids from San Diego who had traveled to Delano to deliver food and clothes for the striking grape pickers. At the picket line outside the Delano City Council chambers, he remembered later, the marchers paraded in the dust and heat where they had been for hours. They were there that day following an incident in which a strikebreaker had beaten a farmworker. Residing in the jail that afternoon, however, was not the strikebreaker but the farmworker, who was charged with instigating the trouble.

Shortly after the group of students arrived, they, along with the picketers, were suddenly the object of attack by local teenagers gunning past them in pickup trucks, shouting "Outside Agitators" and "Commies" and hurling rocks.

"Our side prevailed that day," Foster said.

> The jailed farm worker was released and there was a little celebration back at the union office. Chavez greeted us in a buoyant mood. As he stepped forward to shake my hand I remember thinking: But he's so small He was quiet, demure even, speaking in a voice so soft you had to strain to hear him. After all the shouted, hateful threats that had been aimed at us, Chavez's calm was a salve. He carried himself with dignity, and his embrace that day felt like a benediction.[21]

Despite the devastating assassinations, despite the threats to his own life and the intimidation of his fellow farmworkers, despite the grueling days and nights of planning and meetings and travel, Chavez continued on, mixing his remarkable tenacity with a sense of serenity.

"The consumer boycott is the only open door in the dark corridor of nothingness down which farm workers have had to walk for many years," Chavez said. "It is a gate of hope through which they expect to find the sunlight of a better life for themselves and their families."[22]

Throughout 1969, shipments of California table groups were stopped by strikes in Boston, New York, Philadelphia, Chicago, Detroit, Montreal, and Toronto. In some British ports, dockworkers refused to unload grapes. Chavez had established strong working groups, especially in Pennsylvania, New York, Michigan, and Illinois, where young union leaders began to make names for themselves for their own work—Eliseo Medina in Chicago, Jessica Govea in Toronto, and Al and Elena Rojas in Michigan. Across the country, demonstrations, some numbering several hundred people, called attention to the strike.

Robert F. Kennedy's support for the boycott seemed to open the door for other political endorsements. A number of Democratic senators and congressmen now spoke openly in favor of the boycott. Vice President Hubert Humphrey pledged to Chavez that he would push for legislation to support the rights of farm laborers to organize. "I want to make it clear," Humphrey wrote, "that I do endorse your efforts and I hope you will feel free to use that endorsement ... in any way you feel will serve *La Causa*."[23]

After the union declared a boycott on Safeway, the largest chain grocery store in the West, the company fought back. Not only did they refuse to take grapes off the shelves, they hired a large public relations firm to launch a $2 million campaign to convince the public that it was their right to buy California grapes. The public had the right, certainly, to buy the grapes; however, much of the public was listening to Chavez and the union and not to the advertising blitz.

In September, Chavez had recovered sufficiently from his fast and his chronically painful back to embark on a seven-week, nationwide tour. In November he testified before a Senate committee that the union has "clear evidence that growers are poisoning workers and contaminating table grapes by the increasing use of pesticides."[24] Chavez would increasingly fight the growers over the pesticide issue as *La Causa* moved forward in its various campaigns.

Chavez also addressed an open letter to the grape industry that the union circulated in various press media. His plea was to recognize workers of the fields as full members of the human community, entitled to the respect and rights due all men, women, and children. He wrote,

> The men and women who have suffered and endured much and not only because of our abject poverty but because we have been kept poor. The color of our skins, the languages of our cultural and native origins, the lack of formal education, the exclusion from the democratic process, the numbers of our slain in recent wars—all these burdens generation after generation have sought to demoralize us, to break our human spirit. But God knows we are not beasts of burden, we are not agricultural implements or rented slaves, we are men. And mark this well ... we are men locked in a death struggle against man's inhumanity to man in the industry that you represent. And this struggle itself gives meaning to our life and ennobles our dying.[25]

On July 29, 1970, with the grape growers realizing that the boycott was having a definite deleterious impact both financially and in the eyes of the public, more than 20 growers, led by John Giumarra Jr., signed a historic pact with Chavez's United Farm Workers Organizing Committee.

It had been five years since the union had struck the vineyards of the San Joaquin Valley. Hundreds of farm workers and union leaders mingled with representatives of the growers at the union's headquarters in Delano. This was a day for which Chavez had labored for so long, a day for the *campesinos*, the workers of the field, their backs bent and pained by years of labor, their hands roughed and skin weathered like leather. Today, many of their black eyes filled as Chavez, along with the growers signed the document that gave their union formal representation.

Wearing a white ceremonial Filipino shirt to honor the Filipino American vineyard workers who began the walkouts in 1965, Chavez thanked the millions of people who proved that social justice could be achieved through nonviolent action. "We said from the beginning," Chavez remarked, "that we were not going to abandon the fight, that we would stay with the struggle if it took a lifetime, and we meant it."[26]

The contract called for a wage of $1.80 plus 20 cents for each box picked. Before the strike, the workers made approximately $1.10 an hour. In addition, growers would begin to contribute to a health plan and the agreement included stringent safety requirements on the use of pesticides.

For the workers this was not merely a victory for wages and better working conditions; for them, the battle was for dignity and for affirmation. On this day, as they jubilantly sang the songs of *La Causa*, as they sang in Spanish *"Nosotros Venceremos"*—the civil rights anthem "We Shall Overcome"—as they shouted the slogans of *"Viva La Huelga!"*, they were asserting newly won respect.

NOTES

1. "Meany Acclaims Coast Farm Pact," *New York Times*, 4 April 1967, p. 25.

2. "Farm Union Pins Its Hopes on Victory in Coast Grape Strike," *New York Times*, 2 October 1967, p. 43.

3. Ibid.

4. "A Farm-Bred Unionist: Cesar Estrada Chavez," 11 March 1968, p. 22.

5. "The Little Strike That Grew to *La Causa*," *Time* (4 July 1969), 17.

6. Ibid., 19.

7. Susan Ferriss and Ricardo Sandoval, *The Fight in the Fields: Cesar Chavez and the Farmworkers Movement* (Orlando, FL: Paradigm Productions, 1997), 140.

8. Jacques Levy, *Cesar Chavez: Autobiography of La Causa,* http://chavez. cde.ca.gov/ModelCurriculum/Teachers/Lessons/Resources/Documents/Chavez_ Biography_by_Levy.PDF.

9. Ibid.

10. "The Little Strike That Grew," 19.

11. Cesar E. Chavez, "The Mexican-American and the Church," http://www. wccusd.k12.ca.us/stc/Waysofthinking/append/chavezspeech2.htm.

12. "A Shared Bond: Cesar Chavez and Martin Luther King, Jr.," http://www. cesarechavezfoundation.org/.

13. "Robert F. Kennedy Conference, November 18, 2000," John F. Kennedy Presidential Library and Museum, http://www.jfklibrary.org/forum_rfk_conf.html.

14. Ibid.

15. *New York Times,* 11 March 1968.

16. "Robert F. Kennedy Conference."

17. "Excerpts from Quotes in the Chavez-Kennedy Commemorative Photo Exhibit, May 28, 1998," http://www.ufw.org/cecrfk.htm.

18. "I've Been to the Mountaintop," delivered 3 April 1968, in Memphis, Tennessee, http://www.americanrhetoric.com/speeches/mlkivebeentothemountain-top.htm.

19. Cesar Chavez, "Lessons of Dr. Martin Luther King, Jr., January 12, 1990," http://aztlan.net/cesarMLK.htm.

20. "Excerpts from Quotes."

21. Douglas Foster, "Elegy for a Hero," http://www.pbs.org/itvs/fightfields/ cesarchavez2.html.

22. Claire Peterson and Susana Diaz, "Exploring the United Farm Workers' History," http://library.thinkquest.org/26504/History.html.

23. Ellen Grace, "*La Causa para La Rasa:* The Educative Processes and Development of Knowledge in the United Farm Workers from 1962 to 1970," http://scholar.lib.vt.edu/theses/available/etd-3198-194743.

24. *Los Angeles Times,* 26 September 1969.

25. Cesar Chavez, "An Open Letter to the Grape Industry," 1969, http:// www.tuhsd.k12.az.us/Compadre_HS/servicelearning/AnOpenLettertotheGrape Industry.doc.

26. "26 Grape Growers Sign Accord; Boycott Nears End," *New York Times,* 30 July 1970, p. 19.

Chapter 7

BATTLEGROUND IN THE FIELDS

THE LETTUCE STRIKE AND BOYCOTT

On July 29, 1970, with the jubilant singing of farmworkers celebrating their new labor contracts still reverberating around Delano's union head-quarters, Cesar Chavez retired to his office. He had immediate work to do in preparing for the next battle.

In California's Salinas Valley, Chavez had recently learned, lettuce growers were attempting to avoid the same fate that befell the grape grow-ers. A narrow, fertile pocket of about 100 miles, Salinas Valley produces a lion's portion of the nation's vegetables—iceberg lettuce, broccoli, arti-chokes, celery, carrots, and other produce that shows up on kitchen tables across America. It is the birthplace of the celebrated American writer John Steinbeck, who chronicled the challenges and personal travails and occasional triumphs of Depression-era America's migrant poor in *The Grapes of Wrath* and other novels. It had been in Salinas where growers in 1936 had brought in hired thugs to quell labor organizing and made the verdant valley into a battlefield.

And now, in 1970, almost every lettuce grower in the area had begun signing union contracts with the Teamsters Union, agreements far more favorable to the growers than any contracts they could possibly work out with Chavez's union, the United Farm Workers Organizing Committee (UFWOC). The growers and the Teamsters signed the contracts secretly without consulting with the workers. Once again the Teamsters were attempting to add to their already considerable power by destroying Chavez's union. Once again, a segment of California's agribusiness industry, this time the lettuce growers, was attempting to stop Chavez in his tracks.

With its identification with the civil rights movement and with Democratic politicians such as Robert F. Kennedy and others, the Chavez movement was a special irritant to most Republican Party leaders, from President Richard Nixon on down. Its success was especially irritating to Governor Ronald Reagan, the former movie actor who had taken over the California governorship a few years earlier and who enjoyed the strong support of the state's agribusiness establishment. The Reagan administration conducted a mean-spirited attack on Chavez and his union, a campaign tinted with ethnic resentment and personal mockery of Chavez himself. During the grape boycott, Reagan frequently found it convenient to have himself photographed popping a grape into his mouth or offering grapes to reporters and other visitors. He called the grape contracts "tragic."[1]

Republicans were more determined than ever to rid California and the country of this increasingly powerful movement they insisted was tainted with left-wing propagandists and liberal do-gooders. In this effort to put down the fledgling movement, the Teamsters, the only major union now clearly on the side of the Republican Party, was more than eager to assist.

The campaign against the farmworkers' union fired the emotions of Chavez. In his office, he told a reporter that the union was again ready for a confrontation. "Those growers in Salinas really did us a favor," said one of Chavez's lieutenants. "Now we're the underdogs again."[2] Chavez told his associate to pack his bag; they were going to Salinas.

Chavez had not planned to take on the lettuce growers so quickly after the grape boycott, but the collusion between the Teamsters and the companies forced his hand. He called a strike against the lettuce ranches in Salinas. On the third day, an estimated 10,000 workers had already walked out of the fields and the fight was on.

When the growers went to court seeking an injunction against the strike, Chavez responded by upping the ante. As he had done in the case of the grape pickers fight, he decided to call a nationwide boycott of all lettuce produced by growers who did not have contracts with his union.

Chavez told a reporter that he was optimistic about the farmworkers' struggle. He said that the movement had become an instrument through which poor farmworkers could wind their way out of a cycle of poverty. He said, "I contend that not only the American public, but people in general throughout the world will respond to a cause that involves injustice. It's just natural to want to be with the underdog. In a boxing match, however popular the champion may be, if he begins to really get the other guy and beat him up bad, there is a natural tendency to go with the underdog." This struggle between his infant union and Republicans, Teamsters, and big business, he said, was "not a contest between two people or a team but a contest between a lot of people who are poor and others who are wealthy."[3]

Soon, for more than 100 miles in each direction, from Monterey County to Santa Cruz, the red flags waved. "It looked like a revolution," said Jerry Cohen, the general counsel for the strikers. "And some of these right-wing growers thought it was."[4]

The growers hired guards armed with shotguns to protect their ranches. Teamster enforcers, some wielding baseball bats, walked the lines, taunting the strikers. In the fields the mood became increasingly tense and the poor were on the receiving end of violence. On August 25, Jerry Cohen was beaten unconscious by Teamsters enforcers. On the same day, one of growers drove a tractor into a crowd of picketers and demolished two pickup trucks owned by the workers.

On August 29, a caravan of trucks and cars forced a union member to drive his car off the road. He was soon surrounded and beaten and his wife, trying to prevent the beating, was hit in the face. At another picket line in Gonzales, California, a striker was shot in the leg. And in November, a dynamite explosion blew away the windows and door of a union office in Hollister, California.

The tensions took on obvious racial and ethnic tones. Truckers sped around the Salinas area waving American flags and cursing the Aztec eagle. Wives of company owners and other antiunion protestors paraded along Salinas streets in counterdemonstrations, also waving American flags.

As the chaos escalated, police were now quick to brandish guns. When Chavez tried to present these cases in the San Mateo Superior Court as grounds for an injunction to prevent further violence, his attorneys were nearly laughed out of court. Judge Melvin Cohn referred to them as representatives of Cesar Chavez, "star of radio, TV, and newspapers."[5]

Despite his avowed optimism about the struggle ahead, Chavez, on December 4, 1970, went to jail. The charge was contempt of court after he refused to call off the nationwide boycott of lettuce. As he walked into the jail in Salinas, a huge crowd of 2,000 farmworkers gathered outside, many carrying the red and black flag of the union with its fierce eagle and waving banners of La Causa. Carrying a bullhorn, Larry Itliong, one of the vice presidents of the union, spoke to the crowd: "Today shows us that the growers can utilize their influence with the courts and the government to destroy the right of the poor and the farm workers to have a decent life.

But we won't let them stop us." As Itliong concluded his remarks and the crowd knelt to pray, one observer whispered to another, "This was the one credential Chavez didn't have. Now he's been in jail, too."[6]

On Christmas Eve, 1970, Chavez walked out of the Salinas jail. By the time of his release, he had reenergized the farmworkers' struggle. Once again, in attempting to thwart the farmworkers' movement, Chavez's enemies had given him greater visibility on the national scene and an increasingly sympathetic ear from large segments of the American population who saw in the union an effort to help individuals who were being crushed under society's weight. Visitors from across the country, learning of his jailing, arrived in Salinas to show support. Gathering night after night at the jail, strikers found among themselves renewed aggressiveness to carry on. Each attack by the Teamsters, the growers, the political establishment, and the courts seemed more to rally the troops than to demoralize them.

In 1971, Cesar and his family and some of the union's administrators moved from Delano to Keene, California, located southwest of Bakersfield in the foothills of the Tehachapi Mountains. A collection of wood frame buildings that had formerly been a tuberculosis sanitarium, sheltered from the noise and commotion in Delano, the site was a perfect place for Chavez to spend time physically recovering from his grinding self-imposed pace and for the union leaders to retreat for planning and strategy meetings. It was also a place where recruits from around the country could meet with union leaders and receive training. The credit union, clinic, and hiring hall remained in Delano. Chavez called the new headquarters "La Paz," a shortened version of Nuestra Senora de la Paz, or Our Lady of Peace.

It was during this period that Chavez led the UFWOC into a formal charter agreement with the AFL-CIO. The union now became an official affiliate of the AFL-CIO, and its name was now the United Farm Workers of America (UWF).

In 1971 Guadalupe Gamboa, a young student from Washington State who was imbued with the spirit of the farmworkers' movement, visited Chavez and the others at La Paz shortly after they had moved in. The young man was there to be counseled in the art of organizing. It was through the training and encouragement of organizers such as Gamboa that the union spread its influence across the United States, especially in heavy agricultural areas such as Washington.

"It was a big complex," Gamboa later remembered,

It had over three hundred acres. So we went there and we were trained for about two or three—I think it was two days. Fred Ross, Sr., who is the person who trained Cesar on how to organize, and Cesar himself spent two days talking to us, just telling us the basics of organizing and giving us a history of how the organizing techniques that they had used very successfully in organizing farm workers had developed. The main organizing technique that the union was using at that time and that we still use is called the house meeting—house meeting campaign drive, where you would rely on other workers themselves to help you organize a community.[7]

The main idea, Gamboa remembered, was to leave the house meeting only after convincing others to hold their own house meetings. Through these chains of meetings, the union membership spread throughout the community.

By 1971, the union had won pivotal contracts. Dolores Huerta, for example, had bargained a very favorable contract from InterHarvest, a lettuce and vegetable giant with ties to Central America. Not only did the increase in wage to $2.10 far exceed anything that the Teamsters had been able to offer farmworkers, but Huerta also negotiated an agreement by the company to eliminate the use of DDT and other dangerous pesticides that Chavez and the union had begun to denounce.

Some of UFW's most critical battles lay ahead. But Chavez and the farmworkers' union were now established players on a much larger stage than the fruit and vegetable valleys of California.

Especially in the large cities such as Los Angeles and Chicago, young Mexican Americans now followed closely the drama being played out in the fields of California. A new generation of young people looked to reclaim the pride and heritage of their culture. They began to use the name "Chicano," a term once used as a racial slur against Mexican Americans. They took the name as a gesture of political defiance and ethnic pride. One of their heroes was Cesar Chavez.

NONVIOLENCE AND THE VIETNAM WAR

As did his spiritual mentor, Martin Luther King Jr., Chavez became an outspoken opponent of the war in Vietnam. The U.S. effort in Southeast Asia to prevent the spread of communism was now slogging through another year of killing and dying and the protest movements spawned by its escalating toll on American prestige, money, and lives was growing ever larger.

In 1970, the antiwar protest movement became firmly rooted in the Mexican American community. On August 29, 1970, at a demonstration in East Los Angeles, more than 30,000 protestors, led by an organization called the National Chicano Moratorium, focused the nation's attention on the fact that Mexican American youth were being drafted and killed in disproportionate numbers.

Herman Baca, one of the young leaders of the Moratorium, later recalled the growing hostility of the Mexican American community to the war. "Those of us who were involved in the Chicano movement," he said, "recoiled in anger and called for protests against the government's policy in sending our young men to die in Vietnam ... the white racist system had made Chicano[s] strangers in their own land, placed them last in jobs, educations and rights, but had always placed them first to die in its wars."[8]

In a letter written to the Moratorium Committee, Chavez said, "It is now clear to me that the war in Vietnam is gutting the soul of our nation. Of course we know the war to be wrong and unjustifiable, but today we see that it has destroyed the moral fiber of the people."[9]

Many of the Chicano Moratorium participants were teargassed and beaten that day in Los Angeles by police. One prominent Mexican American journalist, Ruben Salazar, was killed.

Marc Grossman, an early Chavez organizer, said that Chavez's belief in nonviolence was not absolute. "He would quote Gandhi. If the choice were between only violence and cowardice," Grossman said, "Chavez would choose violence.... Nevertheless, Chavez was very much against the Vietnam War which he saw as foolish, morally devastating, and extremely costly in the lives of the poor."[10]

In 1971, Chavez's antiwar stance took a more personal direction. Fernando Chavez, Cesar's eldest son, decided to refuse induction as a draftee into military service. Citing his long-held belief in nonviolence, he asked to be classified a conscientious objector and excused from serving in the war.

Fernando was arrested for avoiding the draft. When the 22-year-old appeared in federal court in Fresno, California, he said that he was morally opposed to war and could not bring himself to kill another human being. His father testified at the trial. He talked about the religious upbringing of his children and how he and Helen, both through their words and lives, had tried to show that violence was unnecessary to resolve disputes. After three days the court concluded that the draft board had acted precipitously in the case of Chavez and had not allowed him due process in making his case for conscientious objector status.

Later, when looking back on those tense days in his own life, Fernando said that his father had told him, "If you are willing to do that for your convictions, not only will people respect you, but you will respect yourself." The charge to his son was both Cesar Chavez's philosophy and his way of living.[11]

A FIGHT IN ARIZONA

In 1972 Chavez went back to his home state for a fight. In the Arizona statehouse in Phoenix, lawmakers were arguing over a measure that had been introduced to outlaw boycotts and strikes during the harvest season. Some members of the Arizona legislature were determined to prevent in their own state what they saw as a disaster in California—the rise of the farmworker union.

Chavez hoped to meet with Arizona governor Jack Williams, a Republican, to plead the case against the legislation, along with other labor leaders in the state. On the other side, Arizona's growers saw the bill as a chance to win a significant victory in the legislative arena, one that would stall, if not kill, efforts to forge a significant farmworkers' union in the state.

Williams had no desire to see Chavez or any other labor leader. So anxious was he to sign the bill that he ordered a highway patrolman to deliver it to his office just 45 minutes after it had passed the legislature so that he could sign it immediately. Historians of Arizona vainly looked for any other instances in the state's history that a governor went to such lengths to approve a piece of legislation. The gesture was a crude, back of the hand slap to Arizona's farmworkers, and Chavez was furious. Governor Williams, secure in his tight political circles with the Republican establishment in Arizona and confident of his own political security, had unwittingly lit a fuse. The blast would be heard nationwide.

Chavez decided to attack with a tested strategy—he went on a "fast for love." On May 11, he retired to a small room in the Santa Rita Center in South Phoenix, away from the political establishment and in the Mexican American community. Into Arizona streamed news reporters from the *New York Times* and other national newspapers and magazines. Into Arizona came Coretta Scott King; Joseph Kennedy, the eldest son of Robert Kennedy; and folk singer Joan Baez. *La Causa* was now focused on a state not used to this kind of national publicity.

Chavez fasted for 24 days, at which time his doctors, noticing an erratic heartbeat, feared for his life. On June 5, 1972, he ended the fast with a mass attended by some 5,000 people from throughout Arizona and several other states. This mass was not held in South Phoenix. In a bold move to attract even greater attention and to make a statement about the rising power of the movement, it was held in Phoenix's most

popular gathering spot, the Del Webb Townhouse, not exactly a center
for labor organizers. Ending his fast with communion, Chavez explained
his actions with these words:

> The fast was meant as a call to sacrifice for justice and as a reminder
> of how much suffering there is among farm workers. In fact, what
> is a few days without food in comparison to the daily pain of our
> brothers and sisters who do backbreaking work in the fields under
> inhuman conditions and without hope of ever breaking their cycle
> of poverty and misery. What a terrible irony it is that the very people
> who harvest the food we eat do not have enough food for their own
> children.[12]

Through the attention of the fast and the gathering of hundreds of
workers to the state, Chavez sought to overturn the law and to impeach
Governor Williams and remove him from office. To achieve the latter,
the workers needed to collect enough signatures in a petition campaign
to call for a new election. Although about 160,000 signed up, the state's
attorney general declared most of them to be invalid. The recall effort
failed and the farm-labor law remained in effect.

Nevertheless, while petitioning the state, Chavez's workers also conducted a voter registration drive in the Mexican American communities.
Two years later, those thousands of voters streamed to the polls to elect a
new governor and other state officials. For the first time, several Mexican
American candidates came away victorious, including Raul Castro, the
first Hispanic governor in the history of Arizona.

It was in the Arizona campaign that the words "Sí, se puede" (It can
be done) became another rallying cry for the farmworkers. At an early
planning meeting before the fast, several of Chavez's lieutenants were
worried that in this fight Chavez had taken on a greater task than could
be accomplished in a state so traditionally conservative and controlled by
agribusiness interests. They reportedly said to Chavez, "No se puede." The
farmworkers leader spun those words around.

It was also in the Arizona campaign that the union made its first significant progress in eliminating from the lives of the farmworkers el cortito,
the dreaded short-handled hoe. The success resulted from the efforts of two
individuals who were in Phoenix when Chavez carried on his protest.

During those days, Chavez consulted Earl Wilcox, who later served in
the Arizona legislature and tried for two years to convince Arizona lawmakers to pass a bill outlawing the two-foot long tool that made it necessary for farmworkers to bend over in a contorted position while working

in the fields. Although he persuaded nearly 300 people to testify before the legislature, conservative lawmakers managed to quell the effort.

The defeat did not stop Wilcox. He decided to work around the legislature and approach the Arizona Industrial Commission, the state agency that monitored occupational safety and health issues. Wilcox had a friend at the commission—Daniel Ortega, who was a student at Arizona State University when Chavez fasted in Phoenix. By a vote of 5 to 0 the commission eliminated the short-handled hoe by regulation. It was, Wilcox said later, his proudest moment as a legislator.

Daniel Ortega said that Chavez represented to him what activism is all about. "My father and mother and brothers and sisters and I all worked the fields," he said. "We used to drive out to Tempe on Sundays to see my grandparents," he says, "and when we drove by ASU, I'd always say, 'I'm going to go to school there someday.' My mother would later tell me it hurt her heart to hear me say that because she knew I'd never get there because we had no money. But, of course, she didn't tell me that. She'd tell me, 'Of course you can.'" Not only did Ortega get a degree from ASU, but so did six of his brothers and sisters. All that momentum, he said, started during those student days when Ortega met Chavez and began to work for La Causa.[13]

LIVING WITH THE FEAR

Rees Lloyd, who served as an attorney for Chavez for twenty years, wrote of the constant apprehension of many of Chavez's friends about his safety. "Cesar Chavez received death threats by the dozens," Lloyd wrote. "We had to bodyguard him wherever he went. In the fields, he walked through phalanxes of hired thugs at strike sites in the fields. He was spit on, threatened, cursed, struck, called a 'dirty little Mexican communist,' and worse. He never flinched. He walked serenely through the vileness, and violence. He appeared to be impervious, without fear. He never wavered. In the cause, or in his commitment to non-violence."[14]

With the nearly incomprehensible tragedy of two assassinations in 1968 still haunting his moves, Chavez did not speak much about the potential violence against himself. He was deeply concerned about the possibility that his own protestors and strikers could be enticed into retaliatory violence. Several such incidents were the principal reason Chavez undertook his first fast.

All around him were the kind of spiteful mobs and scurrilous race-baiting and taunts that could at any time lead to physical clashes. In Detroit, his daughters Linda and Sylvia, on the road to help organize the farmworkers in the Midwest, were doused with a water hose while picketing in the snow.

In the summer of 1971, Chavez was told of some specific information that had been uncovered by the federal Bureau of Alcohol, Tobacco, and Firearms in Washington about a possible plot to assassinate the labor organizer. The information had come from an informant in Bakersfield, California, who was told that a drug dealer had been given $25,000 to hire a hit man to kill Chavez. Behind the plot, the informant claimed, were several individuals involved with the California fruit and vegetable industries.

Armed with this information, the federal agents set up a sting operation to see if they could corroborate the story. In tape recordings made of the drug dealer, the agents heard the same kind of information they had received from the informer. The planned hit on Chavez was on.

Later, while heading toward Salinas where Chavez was to speak, the alleged hit man, Buddy Gene Prochnau, was arrested in connection with a contract murder in Visalia, California. He was later convicted for the crime and sentenced to life in prison.

Although the Bureau of Alcohol, Tobacco, and Firearms dropped the investigation after the apprehension of Prochnau, both the U.S. Justice Department and the California State Attorney General's Office conducted limited investigations to attempt to find out who may have been willing to pay for the hit on Chavez. The investigations plodded on and were finally dropped altogether, leaving many Chavez supporters with the strong conviction that both federal and California sta te authorities had engaged in a cover-up.

The news of the plot against his life only slightly curtailed Chavez's activities in the summer of 1971. At first he did not believe there was such a plot in the works; later, he realized it was likely true.

Still very much concerned that the plan to kill Chavez was alive or that other plans were being concocted, Jerry Cohen, legal counsel for Chavez, told the *New York Times*, "Maybe all we got was a reprieve. We still have people out there who put up a substantial sum of money. They could be looking for another hit man."[15]

BATTLING THE TEAMSTERS

The International Brotherhood of Teamsters was the only major working-class organization to support the Republican Party in the post–World War II period. It was also the only labor union to support the bracero program that brought Mexican workers to the United States to work in fields for limited periods of time. Although the Teamsters had attempted to organize field hands, its efforts had little to do with the interests of those workers; its motivation was to insure that the truckers, their main constituency, would never be without fruits and vegetables to transport. The main interest of the Teamsters in signing up farmworkers was to ensure that they never went on strike. The interests of the Teamsters, therefore, were also those of the growers and those of the Republican Party. In the eyes of Chavez's union, it was this hydra-headed foe that had to be slain for the farmworkers to get a fair deal.

In an open letter published in the major newspapers across the country, Chavez wrote of the alliance of the Teamsters with the Republican Party and their corporate business friends and their attempts to destroy the farmworkers' union. In his letter, Chavez quoted Charles Colson, a Nixon aide. Writing to an official in the justice department, Colson said, "... But we must stick to our position. The Teamsters Union is now organizing the area and will probably sign up most of the grape growers this coming spring and they will need our support against the UFW."[16]

In 1973, Chavez's assumptions proved correct. When the farmworkers' three-year contracts were up for renegotiation, most of the grape growers quickly signed contracts with the Teamsters. Chavez responded with another strike. Beginning in farms in the Coachella and San Joaquin valleys, approximately 10,000 farm workers walked out of the fields.

This time the strikers faced increasing strong-arm tactics. Many of the striking farmworkers were arrested or beaten. It was not the attackers, however, who went to jail. Throughout the summer local judges, with close personal and political ties to the growers, issued injunctions limiting legitimate strike activity. Local sheriffs, instead of acting as peacemakers, often joined the Teamsters and other strikebreakers in creating melees to disperse strikers. Thousands of farmworkers, among them women, children and older men, were sprayed with mace, beaten, and jailed. Some needed hospitalization.

The FBI received numerous stories about the violence being meted out to farm workers. One citizen wrote to William Ruckelshaus, acting director of the FBI, "Equal protection under the law is being reduced to a myth in Coachella Valley California. No manifestation of local law enforcement is willing to provide proper protection to the members of the United Farm Workers, to individual farm workers, and to other individuals, who are working to better the conditions of life for some of the most oppressed working people in the country. Goon squads of thugs of engaged in terror tactics, physical force, and violence in an effort to totally destroy the United Farm Workers program, no matter what the cost." Seemingly unconcerned about the confrontations in California's fields, the FBI ignored this and other pleas to intercede.[17]

An FBI agent in the field got first-hand testimony from a farmworker who was approached by three Teamsters driving a Lincoln Continental. "They said they were Teamsters," the worker remembered. "We did not even know at that time what a Teamster was. They said they were here to 'knock some wetbacks heads in;' then they also said that they were 'going to make some other wetbacks work in the fields in the sun so they would get strokes and die.'" The worker told the agent that the men in Lincoln said the workers should join the Teamsters or face the consequences. "They told us to watch the news the next day and we did and like they had said there was going to be violence and heads bust open sure enough the news reported some incidents."[18]

Susan Drake, one of Chavez's long-time workers, wrote,

> Several union brothers and a female volunteer were killed during the strikes, but we did not kill. One morning in 1973 on the Lamont picket line, I watched three or four greasy goons attack the strikers. Not one of our 75 people raised a fist or knife when the blood flowed. Nonviolence kept strikers on the picket lines instead of in jail. It was nearly impossible that day and many others to hold our tempers to words. Nonviolence proved an effective organizing tool to set United Farm Workers apart from the bullying unions so familiar to some growers during labor strikes in the 1930's.[19]

Dorothy Day, a long-time influential and controversial Catholic pacifist, joined other protestors in support of Chavez in 1973. When she arrived on July 30, there had been mass arrests of farmworkers who were defying the injunction against picketing. On August 1, she wrote in her diary:

> A very hot drive down the valley to Delano today, arriving as strike meeting ended. Today many Jesuits were arrested. Also sisters who had been attending a conference in San Francisco. Mass in the evening at Bakersfield, ended a tremendous demonstration, flag-carrying Mexicans—singing, chanting, marching—and when the Mass began there were so many people that it was impossible to kneel, but there was utter silence.[20]

The following day Chavez arrived and spoke to the protestors about the injunction and arrests. By that evening, Day herself was in custody. "Here we are," she wrote, "99 women strikers including 30 sisters, 50 men strikers including two priests. This is a 640-acre farm and can accommodate 300. Now greatly overcrowded. During crucial meetings between Cesar Chavez and Teamsters the sisters all signed up for a night of prayer, taking two-hour shifts all through the night, and the Mexican women all knelt along the tables in the center and prayed the rosary together."[21]

On August 14, 1973, striker Nagi Daifullah, a 24-year-old Arab from Yemen, was beaten; he died from a massive brain hemorrhage shortly thereafter. A mile-long parade of several thousand marchers with black flags and black arm-bands and ribbons walked to his funeral service. Along with psalms and other Catholic rituals, Moslem chants, and Arab music, the huge crowd, most of them Roman Catholic, stood together.

Two days after Nagi Daifullah's death, while picketing at the Giumarra Vineyards, 60-year-old Juan de la Cruz of Delano, marching with his wife, Maximina, was shot through the chest and killed by a sniper firing from a speeding pickup truck. Mass was offered by a Catholic bishop who had come to the United States from Ecuador. Neither of the killings resulted in convictions.

One of Chavez's supporters later remembered Chavez as a most wily judge of human nature and the tactics of confrontation. "On one memorable occasion," he wrote, Chavez "was locked up in a rural jail for allegedly violating a picketing injunction in a strike. The arrest generated great support for the strike. The authorities, therefore, told Cesar he was free to leave. He refused. They ordered him to leave. He refused, and sent an order to the lawyers: 'Keep me in jail.' Thus, the Sheriff battled in court to throw Cesar out of jail, not in. Cesar, meanwhile, organized the inmates of the jail; violence ceased out of respect for him; and when he finally agreed to leave, it was the cleanest jail in California. Hundreds of cheering supporters greeted him when he finally agreed to leave the jail."[22]

Nevertheless, by the end of the summer of 1973, the United Farm Workers, despite its heroic efforts, seemed destined to fail under the onslaught of its opponents. Three years earlier, the union had signed contracts with approximately 150 vineyards, including the major growers in the United States. In the short space of its existence, the organization had founded for its members medical clinics, a credit union, a health plan, death benefit programs, and a retirement village. Most importantly, it had achieved for many Mexican American workers a new sense of dignity, that they were to be treated not merely as farm implements but as fellow Americans.

But now, against the strong-armed, aggressive force of the Teamsters, backed by their political friends in power, Chavez's union had only a token number of contracts with the growers. The membership of the organization had shrunk from a high of 40,000 to fewer than 10,000. It seemed to most outside observers that the halcyon days of the United Farm Workers were past.

On September 1, Chavez, despairing over the loss of life and the injuries to his union members, decided to call off the strike. He did not, however, call off the war. Instead, he decided to resume the nationwide boycott. In a letter that was distributed across the country, Chavez pleaded for consumers to back the union in this critical time. "Our small union, poor and struggling to get started, will not be destroyed," he wrote. "Neither the growers, nor the Teamsters, nor the White House has the power to crush our spirit or to overcome the thousands of people who help us because of their faith. You are the crucial element they cannot control ... please boycott *all* grapes and Gallo wines and don't buy or eat iceberg (head) lettuce unless you are sure it bears our label.... Please join with us in our struggle for self-determination and dignity."[23]

Chavez now faced his greatest challenge. His union was nearly broke. Chavez faced formidable enemies and a growing belief that he could not win the war. A San Francisco housewife, who had been an active Chavez supporter since the beginning of the movement, told a reporter in 1974, "I was really a believer. My kids had never even tasted grapes, and for three years I used spinach to make salads. I still wish Chavez well but I'm out of it now ... it wore me out. I worry more now about the price of a head of lettuce than the issue of who picked it."[24]

When the farmworkers' union was in its infancy, television cameras and news reporters scrambled to cover the protest marches and the lines of strikers in the vineyards. It was as if the whole country was watching; indeed, much of it was. The movement had been part of the fervor of change of the late 1960s, along with the civil rights marches and the antiwar crusades. Now, at isolated protest gatherings across the country, small bands of Chavez supporters worked lonely vigils. It was as if no one was watching.

It was this sense of vulnerability and decline in his ranks that Chavez braced himself to attack. He decided to do it with a method used so successfully nearly a decade earlier. He decided to gather his forces for another march.

NOTES

1. "26 Grape Growers on Coast Sign Pact with Union: Reagan Issues Statement," *New York Times*, 30 July 1970, p. 19.

2. "Chavez and His Grape Workers Overcome," *New York Times*, 2 August 1970, p. iv, 2.

3. Bob Fitch, "Tilting with the System," *The Christian Century* (18 February1970), 204.

4. Susan Ferriss and Ricardo Sandoval, *The Fight in the Fields: Cesar Chavez and the Farmworkers Movement* (Orlando, FL: Paradigm Productions, 1997), 170.

5. Jerry Berman and Jim Hightower, "Chavez and the Teamsters," *The Nation* (2 November 1970), 429.

6. "A Defiant Chavez Goes to Jail, Refusing to Halt Lettuce Strike," *New York Times*, 5 December 1970, p. 23.

7. "Interview with Guadalupe Gamboa, April 9, 2003," http://depts. washington.edu/pcls/ufw/guadalupe_gamboa.htm.

8. Herman Baca, "The Day the Police Rioted! Remembering 32 Years Ago," 15 August 2002," http://www.azteca.net/aztec/cmora.html.

9. "Cesar Chavez: A Legacy for Peace, Justice and Non-Violence," *People's Weekly World*, 29 March 2003, http://www.pww.org/article/view/3164/152.

10. O. Ricardo Pimental, "Chavez Saw War as Proof of Failure," *Arizona Republic*, 15 April 2003, p.18.

11. Ibid.

12. Jana Bommersbach, "The Legacy of Cesar," *Phoenix Magazine*, April 2004, http://www.janabommersbach.com/phx-mag-apr04.htm.

13. Ibid.

14. Rees Lloyd, "Cesar Chavez—Remembering an Uncommon Man," http://www.welshamerican.com/cesarchavez.htm.

15. "Informer Says He Was Part of Coast Plot to Kill Cesar Chavez," *New York Times*, 2 January 1972, p. 31.

16. Cesar Chavez, "A Letter from Cesar Chavez," *New York Review of Books*, 31 October 1974, http://www.nybooks.com/articles/9359.

17. Cesar Chavez FBI File, Citizens Action Committee, Jackson, Maine to William Ruckelshaus, 6 July 1973. File can be purchased at http://www.paperlessarchives.com/chavez.html.

18. Ibid., affidavit executed in Lamont, California, 3 August 1973.

19. Susan Drake, "Come, I'd Like You to Meet Cesar Chavez," http://www.cin.org/archives/cinjustann/200304/0008.html.

20. "On Pilgrimage—September 1973," *The Catholic Worker* (September 1973) 1, 2, 6.

21. Ibid.

22. Rees Lloyd.

23. Cesar Chavez, "A Letter from Cesar Chavez."

24. Winthrop Griffith, "Is Chavez Beaten?," *New York Times Magazine* (15 September 1974), 18–20.

Chapter 8

POLITICAL PROWESS

MARCH TO MODESTO

On February 22, 1975, several hundred members of the United Farm Workers (UFW) began a 110-mile march from San Francisco to Modesto, headquarters of the E&J Gallo winery. Other contingents of the march headed out from Stockton and Fresno. Gallo would thus be approached from the north, south, and west, a kind of siege on the winemaker.

The idea was that of Chavez's friend and close associate, Fred Ross. Bitter and defiant over articles in the *New York Times* and *Time* magazine about the apparent faltering state of the farmworkers' movement, Ross suggested to Chavez that they demonstrate once again the clout of the organization and the kind of emotional firepower that they had generated over the years.

This was an organization gaining the allegiance of increasing numbers of workers, Ross believed, and a march on the Gallo company would become a national demonstration of that strength. One of the most visible and well known of the wine companies, Gallo had been in the forefront of those signing up with the Teamsters in defiance of the Chavez union. Almost one of every three bottles of wine sold in the United States each year was produced by Gallo. It was the perfect target.

Although Chavez was at first skeptical about undertaking another high-visibility march, he became convinced that Ross was right. In addition to galvanizing the support of the workers, Chavez realized, the march would generate another flood of national publicity and put to rest any idea that the union was in decline.

In addition, the march could also, Chavez thought, have a very important additional purpose—to stir the political forces in Sacramento to enact legislation that would benefit the farm workers. No longer were Ronald Reagan and his conservative business supporters controlling the governorship of California. The new governor, a liberal Democrat, would be much more sympathetic to *La Causa*.

Jerry Brown, son of former California governor Pat Brown, had studied at a Jesuit Seminary, received a law degree from Yale University, and degrees in Latin and Greek from the University of California, Berkeley. When he took over as California's governor, he immediately began to distance himself from the usual trappings of power. He refused to live in the new governor's mansion and chose, instead, to rent a modest apartment. Instead of being chauffeured around in the governor's limousine, he picked out a Plymouth. He appointed an increased number of women and minority individuals to office, including some of very close friends of *La Causa*, such as LeRoy Chatfield, a former union organizer, who became Brown's director of administration.

The image Brown sought to display from his first days in office was clear. This would be an administration sensitive to the people and not beholden to rich corporate and agribusiness executives. It was a message that Chavez embraced. The union leader was convinced early on that Brown was truly interested in bringing meaningful, progressive change to the state and its workers.

With Brown's ascension to power in Sacramento, Chavez saw enormous political opportunity. While Reagan was in office, the state legislature on three separate occasions sent a bill to his desk granting unemployment insurance for farmworkers. Each time, the bill was struck down by the governor's veto. With Brown in office, such legislation relating to farmworkers would not be treated with such cavalier disdain, Chavez knew. Brown's governorship provided Chavez and his union something they had not had since their earliest days—a real chance to gain in the legislative arena some of the reforms necessary to improve the working conditions for farmworkers.

At first, Chavez had been skeptical that a law could make a substantial difference. Indeed, he feared that the energy of the movement might be drained in a legislative approach. It was Brown himself who argued with vigor that the farmworkers could benefit from concrete farm labor legislation. Brown later remembered his first discussions with Chavez:

My real work with Chavez began shortly after my election as governor when we met in my home in Los Angeles to talk about a proposed farm labor bill. Chavez pulled up to my Laurel Canyon house in an old car with a German shepherd dog named Huelga—Spanish for strike. We talked for several hours about whether the proposed state law or any labor law could actually help farm workers. Chavez repeatedly said that his boycott was a much better organizing tool because the law would always be corrupted by the powerful economic interests that control politics. I argued with him and said that a law would be his best protection. He finally agreed but remained skeptical.[1]

Although a reluctant warrior on the legislative front, Chavez, once convinced of the advantages, poured all his energy into the fight, as he had in other battles throughout his career. But as the marchers left Sacramento, Chavez was not among them. His chronic back problems flared severely, forcing him, for the first time in his life, to be sidelined at the beginning of one of his union's major demonstrations.

A union spokesperson made it clear that the purpose of this march on Modesto was the demand that the farmworkers at Gallo and throughout California be insured of their right to choose which union they wanted to represent them—the Teamsters or the UFW. Chavez was asking for a secret ballot election for farmworkers, not the "sweetheart" deals reached between the Teamsters and the growers for their own respective needs. He was looking for the state legislature and Governor Brown to guarantee through law what the union had not yet been able to achieve through its other pressures.

Over the next several days, farmworkers and their supporters mounted rallies in a number of cities and towns—Oakland, Hayward, Pleasanton, Livermore, Tracy, and Manteca. The marchers stayed in the homes of fellow workers or in churches participating in the march.

On March 1, well over 10,000 members and supporters of the UFW converged in Modesto, over a mile of marchers carrying the union flag and chanting "Chavez sí, Teamsters no; Gallo wine has got to go!" Chavez, who joined the marchers in Modesto, was ebullient over the large turnout and declared, "This should make it clear to Gallo that we're not going away."[2]

CRAFTING LEGISLATION

Shortly after the march, Chavez and his lieutenants met with Governor Brown about the possibility of introducing farmworkers' legislation in the California legislature in the next few months. After a succession of meetings, proposals, and counterproposals, Brown's assistants, with the advice of representatives of the UFW, shaped the outlines of a bill that had the makings of a significant legislative leap forward in establishing legal bargaining rights for migrant laborers in California.

Chavez's close friend LeRoy Chatfield later looked back at those tense days, wondering whether they could craft something acceptable to all sides, whether any piece of legislation acceptable to the UFW could be maneuvered through the state legislature. "I was just straining into my consciousness, anything that I could remember from the past," Chatfield later remembered about Brown. "How this issue was so important to the governor that he wanted to be in very close contact with those working on it, sometimes it just seemed like hours and hours on end. I mean he literally mastered this question of farm labor legislation And he personally made known his views to those who were drafting legislation. I was just really amazed at how quickly and vastly he brought himself in tune with what really goes on out there." Chatfield marveled at Brown's astute political nature, weaving through talks with growers, Teamsters, and the farmworkers' union. He could, Chatfield said, "sense soft points, weakness, if you will."[3]

Through sessions that went on into the early morning hours of both May 3 and May 4, Brown, his assistants, and the UFW negotiators worked to establish the framework that would be acceptable not only to union members and to the state legislature, but would also be a framework that the growers could accept without jeopardizing seriously their own profit potential and reputation.

Finally, when the union leaders decided they had reached a point in the negotiations that represented the minimum they could accept, Brown and his advisors had the outline of a compromise to offer to the state legislators and to the growers. The outline of the bill essentially, for the first time in California history, granted migratory and farm labor workers the right to vote in secret ballot elections for union representation.

On Sunday, May 4, Brown and his advisors summoned growers and their representatives for a meeting on the legislation. Because of the crucial demands of the current legislative schedule, Brown needed to gain the support of growers and legislators over the next several hours. The meeting with the growers began at midnight and lasted until 3:00 A.M. In those three hours, the growers tentatively agreed to a compromise bill. At 3:00 A.M. Brown and his staff began to call to state legislators to persuade them to introduce the bill in the form he had worked out with the UFW and the growers. By 10:30 A.M., May 5, Brown was confident enough about the bill that he made a final call—to Cesar Chavez, at his headquarters near Bakersfield.

Chavez that morning was previewing the film *Fighting for Our Lives*, a documentary on the 1973 strike. From Brown's office, with some loud-speakers attached to his phone, the governor and the growers discussed the bill section by section with Chavez. Finally, Brown asked Chavez if he could support the bill. The union leader said yes.

For farmworkers, the passage of California's Agricultural Labor Relations Act was a legislative triumph of profound consequences, not necessarily for the economic gains it immediately afforded the workers, but for the power it conferred on them. It was no less than the first bill of rights for farmwork-ers in the continental United States, protecting the right of farmworkers to unionize and boycott, and guaranteeing secret ballots in union elections.

Up until now, farmworkers were little more in the capitalist system than rented peasants, forced into the most demeaning conditions of employment and then discarded after harvest seasons. Here was a law that now guaranteed workers the right to choose their own union and to bargain collectively with their employers. Not only was this a source of economic power for the farmworkers' movement, it was a psychological victory of enormous degree. For the thousands of farmworkers who first heard the news, it was an affirmation of their own identity, the worth of their labor, and their right to be treated fairly under the law.

Chavez knew that the passage of the act was only the first legal step in affirming the rights of farmworkers. He knew that the guarantees in the law were not foolproof, that the growers and Teamsters would continue to find ways to evade the law's requirements, that enforcement would be difficult for the state, and that the dodging and weaving of the sides would continue. Growers would use one pretext or another to hold off elections and to stall other negotiations. But Chavez also knew that the movement had made a significant crossing of wild water and, in that, he and his union could take much pride.

ELIMINATING THE SHORT-HANDLED HOE

Roberto Acuna, a farmworker in California, later remembered one of his biggest enemies. "The hardest work would be thinning and hoeing with a short-handled hoe," he said. "The fields would be about a half a mile long. You would be bending and stooping all day. Sometimes I wouldn't have dinner or anything. I'd just go home and fall asleep and wake up just in time to go out to the fields again ... There were times when I felt I couldn't take it any more. It was 105 in the shade and I'd see endless rows of lettuce and I felt my back hurting. I felt the frustration of not being able to get out of the fields."[4]

In 1969 Cesar Chavez declared, "Growers look at human beings as implements. But if they had any consideration for the torture that people go through, they would give up the short-handled hoe."[5]

By 1975, almost all growers, especially outside of California, had abandoned the despised hoe for other tools that allowed workers to stand upright. Nevertheless, California's lettuce growers, insisting that the implement was the fastest and most efficient for the work, continued to require workers to use it. Get rid of the short-handled hoe, the growers argued, and the thinning and weeding would be mishandled, the growers would suffer crop losses, and many of them would go bankrupt. Even when evidence mounted that the tool caused ruptured spinal disks, arthritis, and other serious back injuries, the lettuce growers would not allow other equipment.

Chavez himself suffered debilitating back pain throughout his life, largely because of the twisted posture that the tool demanded. In those early days in the lettuce fields and in weeding sugar-beet fields along the Sacramento River, with the row after row in the searing heat, alone with the hoe, the bag, and the grinding succession of hours hunched in an unforgiving shape, he learned to despise the short-handled hoe as an extension of those who made him use it. It was, he believed, their weapon.

Chavez told civil rights lawyer Mo Jourdane, when they first met in 1967, "Like so many, I wake up in the night with the pain that comes from stooping in the field all day. The short hoe is the nail they use to hang us from the cross."[6]

Jourdane later took a position in the Brown administration's California Rural Legal Assistance program, a state agency whose mission was to provide legal services to individual migrant farmworkers. When he first started his job, one of his coworkers, Hector De La Rosa, told him that if he wanted to help farmworkers in a significant way, he would work to outlaw the short-handled hoe. De La Rosa, who had suffered himself from the effects of such work, decided to give Jourdane a first-hand, quick lesson in cutting lettuce. He took him to a field.

Remembering that lesson, Jourdane later wrote, "I was in pretty good shape back then, but after about an hour, it was torture," he says. "This is why the tool has been dubbed 'la herramienta del Diablo.'" (the devil's instrument).[7]

Jourdane remembered Chavez's personal comment about the hoe years earlier. Now, he was in a position to do something about it. It was the beginning of a personal crusade to end the use of the tool that had meant such physical devastation to thousands and thousands of Mexican American laborers. He needed to gather solid evidence and make a forceful case to agencies in the California state government that had the power to take legal action to outlaw the use of the hoe.

Jourdane and his colleagues, especially Marty Glick, a former civil rights lawyer, first needed to amass strong evidence to convince members of the California Industrial Safety Commission that the short-handled hoe met the definition of an "unsafe hand tool." They also had to show that a different tool could be an acceptable alternative.

They began to quiz physicians about the deleterious effects of working with the instrument. They even consulted Chavez's own doctor. They gathered depositions from workers who had suffered permanent damage. One was a 46-year-old farm worker named Sebastian Carmona. "I came from Texas in 1959 and had never seen a short-handled hoe," said Carmona during his legal battle. "It surprised me, but I thought I'd be able to handle it because it was smaller [than normal]. The first day, when I needed money for my family, I felt a tightness, but I was okay. The second, third, fourth days, it got worse and worse." Carmona recited a litany of back problems that persisted, grew increasingly painful, and made it almost impossible to sleep.[8]

The team worked with a farm organization to test the efficiency of using long-handled hoes for the same work. Contrary to the assumption of most growers and somewhat surprisingly even to the team, the study revealed that not only was the long-handled hoe far less damaging to its user but that it was more efficient. Armed with these findings, Jourdane and his associates, through a succession of appearances before boards, commissions, and other state bureaucratic machinery, built a superior case that the short-handled hoe should be banned from California's agricultural fields.

They also benefited from solid support of Rose Bird, Jerry Brown's secretary of agriculture, the first woman to hold a cabinet-level position in California and one of the few nongrowers ever to hold the agricultural post. A strong supporter of worker safety, Secretary Bird worked assiduously to pave the bureaucratic road toward a formal ban.

Finally, through a Supreme Court ruling and a California administrative ruling by the Brown administration, the short-handled hoe was outlawed. New generations of field workers would never again face what Mo Jourdane called "a flat-out a symbol of oppression—a way to keep control of workers and make them live humbled, stooped-over lives."[9]

THE ROAD AHEAD

However gratifying the victories of 1975—the Agricultural Labor Relations Act and the death of the short-handled hoe, Chavez realized that there would never be a time to quit the fight. Growers would attempt every maneuver they could to exploit loopholes in the law. With each new achievement, each new small step toward equal rights for farmworkers, Chavez became an even more hated target of his political enemies.

He was now 48 years old. The memories of him during this period from friends and acquaintances are of a resilient, dogged, yet unassuming leader. He never became the fiery orator or the powerful presence that marked other reformers and political leaders, but he possessed a quiet magnetism that made people want to follow his example.

Anita Quintanilla, who worked closely with Dolores Huerta in the mid-1970s, remembered that when Chavez appeared in Boston on one occasion with the Kennedy family and other influential Boston political figures, he seemed to take the air of pomposity and self-importance out of the room and fill it with a sense of modest determination.

She remembered visiting the union headquarters at La Paz in the Tehachapi Mountains and accepting Chavez's offer to take a job as his first female security guard. "On these road trips," she said, "I usually rode in the 'suicide car' but one time I occupied the station wagon with Cesar and the driver. As we drove through the central valley of California, Cesar would tell us the UFW history of each town. It was such a pleasure and comfort to hear his soothing voice and such an honor to be privy to his recollections and reflections. He sure loved talking! His German Shepard dogs, Huelga and Boycott, traveled with us and Cesar expressed concern for their comfort. I loved those two dogs and assured Cesar that I was helping take good care of them."[10]

At La Paz, Chavez could find a semblance of relaxation and peace. Jerry Brown remembered the first time he visited Chavez at La Paz. "The place was totally off the beaten path, yet there were hundreds of people around— mostly young and with infectious vitality and enthusiasm. It was clear that the United Farm Workers was a movement. Nuns were typing in the outer office, herb tea was served along with vegetarian food in the common dining room, young volunteers went about their work with a sense of mission."[11]

Chavez found time for amateur photography. He loved to dance and was good at it. He grew chilies in the community garden and could care-fully explain the subtle differences between the various species. He had a cheerful sense of humor. Anita Quintanilla remembered a birthday for Dolores Huerta's oldest daughter. "He managed to convince some of us to get up very early to sing 'Las Mananitas' to her after he served us hot Mexican chocolate with Tequila in it! He went around with a quizzical expression on his face, offering us more to drink. This was one of his less serious ways of celebrating his Mexican heritage."[12]

Reverend Ken Irrgang, a priest and member of the National Farm Worker Ministry, lived and worked for the UFW at La Paz for 12 years and knew Chavez well. He said that Chavez's spiritual grounding was solid, from his earliest days as a boy in Yuma where both his father and mother prayed regularly at home and took the young boy to mass every Sunday and holy day up to the time of his greatest national fame. In all of his time around Chavez, Irrgang said later, he never knew Chavez to deliberately miss mass. At every march and every meeting, Chavez would open with a prayer or a mass.

"On one occasion after I first arrived in La Paz," Irrgang said, "Cesar was in Detroit on a Saturday night speaking engagement. By the time he got back to Los Angeles International Airport it was around 4 A.M. Sunday, and around 6 or 6:30 before he arrived home. And there he was, a couple hours later, in his customary front row seat, ready for Mass. It was only later that I realized I should not have been surprised. He simply never missed Mass—no matter where he was the night or day before."[13]

There was nothing feigned or exaggerated about his religious conviction, Irrgang said, nothing designed to impress onlookers or journalists. In fact, Chavez was very private in his meditation, often going off alone at La Paz early in morning. "Had not meditation been an important part of his life," Irrgang said, "how could he possibly ever have decided to suffer through not one, not two, but three excruciatingly long fasts? You simply don't do things like that without reflecting deeply upon them beforehand."[14]

THE COUNTERATTACKS

It did not take long for Chavez's enemies once again to retaliate. The growers and the Teamsters would use every legal maneuver, political angle, and tactical power play to fight off the effect of the new farmworkers' law. Nevertheless, the first election under the law took place on September 8, 1975, at the Molera Packing Company, a prominent artichoke grower in the Salinas Valley. Before the election, the Teamsters had represented the workers. This time, the workers voted 15 to 0 for the UFW.

The growers quickly mobilized their forces. As laborers throughout the state prepared to vote for labor representation, many of the growers began simply to ignore the law. While giving free access to Teamsters recruiters, they flagrantly chased off UFW organizers. In the first few months alone, the farmworkers' union filed more than a thousand complaints to the state authorities for intimidation and physical assault.

Both Helen Chavez and her daughter Linda Chavez Rodriguez were arrested for trespassing on the grounds of the one of the growers, even though by law they the right to approach workers in the fields. When the police realized they had arrested Chavez's wife and daughter, they immediately released them, fearing a backlash of newspaper publicity.

At one point in the contentious electioneering, members of the Teamsters marched into the office of Governor Brown's Agriculture Labor Relations Board, the agency charged with overseeing the new law, and roughed up two of the bureaucrats, broke a hole in the wall, and pinned Teamsters buttons on one of the men.

Strong evidence emerged that one of the major table grape growers, M. B. Zaninovich, threatened to kill any of his employees who supported Chavez and his UFW union.

In late September 1975, a delegation of Protestant, Catholic, and Jewish clergy and laity from 17 states visited the fields of California to see first hand what was happening under the new law. Vergon Schmid of *The National Catholic Reporter* said the group was "shocked, saddened, and angered" by what they witnessed. They saw armed ranch security guards deny access of union organizers to the field workers; they saw workers threatened and their families threatened; they saw UFW placards and posters torn down; they saw growers intentionally disguise the whereabouts of polling places on election days; they saw ranch foremen force workers to listen to Teamsters spokesmen; they heard workers talk of being beaten and cursed.

In Seattle, seven members of the clergy who went with the delegation returned and held a press conference. They talked about the frustration of witnessing a good law being subverted by lawless elements. "Farm workers are standing up to an overwhelming campaign of intimidation with remarkable bravery," they said.[15]

Despite the raucous and sometimes violent beginnings under the new system, most of the workers who cast votes supported Chavez's union. By 1976, however, the system had still not worked as it was designed. The growers had convinced the state legislature to drain funding for the enforcement of the law through its oversight agency, the Agricultural Labor Relations Board. The growers succeeded, through political manipulation and court challenges, in creating chaos in the state's farmworker labor relations system.

With growers refusing to hold elections and with no state money to prosecute those who ignored the law, labor contracts were held in limbo. Meanwhile, the growers increasingly hired undocumented Mexican immigrants to take the place of the members of Chavez's union in their fields.

Chavez settled on a new tactic. He managed to get on the statewide ballot a controversial referendum, Proposition 14, a measure that would extend the life of the Labor Relations Act, confirming the right of secret ballot and access to workers in the fields by union organizers. The referendum proved to be an enormous gaffe, one of the single most damaging miscalculations Chavez had made since the beginning of the union movement.

Essentially, the ballot referendum was merely asking the state's voters to ratify something already in law. Even if Chavez had been successful in persuading the majority of the state's voters to approve the measure, the reward would be largely ceremonial. Union supporters would still have to fight for the regulatory monies in the state legislature to enforce the provisions of the law.

On the other hand, the growers found Proposition 14 to be a political godsend. In the course of a few months a coalition of growers and Republican Party supporters poured almost $2 million in a media blitz on radio and television to portray the ballot measure in their own terms. Soon, there were ads showing small farmers being besieged in their own homes by ruthless UFW organizers. It was also not lost to Chavez and his supporters that the goons pictured in the ads were Mexican Americans. The growers were playing racial politics with a vengeance.

The fight of the farmworkers for union recognition was something only vaguely familiar to most Californians. The image-makers of the anti-Proposition 14 force did their job chillingly well. On election day, a subdued Chavez and his supporters were stung by a disheartening defeat. For Chavez, however, despair and disillusionment were emotions to be quickly discarded. There was a mountain of work ahead.

THE TEAMSTERS BACK AWAY

For much of the previous decade, Chavez's union had been locked in a viselike struggle for union supremacy among farmworkers. The struggle had been bitter and vindictive, reminiscent of some of the labor struggles in the early days of industrial unionism. For Chavez the struggle had been something of a social and cultural crusade, a movement for dignity and representation by the country's lowliest of workers. For the Teamsters, already a powerful and influential union, the struggle was for power and control. But in March 1977, something rather unusual occurred—peace broke out.

After a number of secret negotiations, Chavez's union and the Teamsters finally reached an agreement. The Teamsters granted the UFW exclusive rights to represent the field workers covered by the Agricultural

Labor Relations Act. The UFW agreed that the Teamsters would have labor jurisdiction in industries surrounding agricultural production, such as canneries, packing sheds, and frozen food operations. Covering not only California but also 11 other western states, the agreement was set for five years. This was clearly a victory for Chavez; indeed, on March 21, 1977, *Newsweek* ran a story entitled "Cesar's Triumph."

Why had the Teamsters, after years of skirmishing and strong-arming, finally decided to negotiate with Chavez, a leader they had grown more and more to despise? Some of the answer lies with the internal turmoil within the Teamsters organization itself. Long under attack for its ties to organized crime, straining under new leadership, and now concerned that the fight with Chavez's union was not only too costly but was hurting their image even further, the Teamsters decided to bargain. Taking on Chavez had been a public relations disaster. Fighting other labor unions was one thing; attacking a movement that had religious, social, and cultural dimensions and a leader who fought with fasts, prayers, and marches was another.

The Teamsters decided that pouring such effort and money into the fight with Chavez had become a losing proposition. In commenting on the agreement with the UFW, Teamsters president Frank Fitzsimmons was quite candid about the image issue. "We now get in a position where we are not accused," he said. "We are not the people suppressing the farm workers."[16]

HOLES IN THE BUILDING BLOCKS

Chavez had taken his infant union on a political roller coaster ride. Through the plunging dips and the upward swoops, they had held on. He knew that the fights by the growers would not cease and that the legislative power in Sacramento would shift over time and that he would lose the advantages that the Brown administration had afforded.

He also realized the extent of the increasing problem of large numbers of new undocumented workers from Mexico who were arriving daily. Growers would brazenly skirt the law, Chavez knew, and would use them in the fields rather than workers from the Chavez union.

He also knew, that with any growing organization, there would be internal struggles within the union leadership itself—personal quarrels, differences in suggested strategies, and the loss of close associates who would continue their careers elsewhere. When the movement was in its infancy, all of Chavez's lieutenants mostly deferred to his leadership without much acrimony or jealousy. Never a skilled administrator or one deftly to delegate leadership roles, Chavez had run the organization with stern control. As the outside battles raged on, close friends and associates held fast to a nearly sacred allegiance to Chavez's guidance. Nevertheless, as the years and the battles went by, some began to question Chavez's decisions and tactics and a few bristled over the lavish attention that Chavez, and Chavez alone, seemed to generate in the press.

The union, which had always been something of a pay-as-you-go venture, began to experience an increasing turnover among its leaders, especially among those individuals who continued to make very small wages or no regular wages at all. Although Chavez established a training school for labor organizers, the demand was quickly exceeding the ability of the school to turn out effective workers. Many of the union's most loyal supporters received no wages for their work in the union. Such an organization can only so long expect workers to keep to a fatiguing schedule with little pay that requires living in spartan conditions, especially if those individuals plan to raise families.

Michael Yates, who worked with Chavez, later remembered a gathering of the union workers at La Paz in March 1977. The group was building a communal garden for the headquarters. After lunch, Chavez began to look back over the recent past—how low he had felt after losing contracts to the Teamsters and how the workers had fought back with unbelievable loyalty and perseverance. He also told the group how he had promised a group of women in Coachella that if the union won back those contracts he would make a pilgrimage to a shrine in Mexico. "As he spoke," Yates remembered, "his voice cracked and he began to cry. I looked around; his daughter was crying and so were many others. I began to cry myself. As the meeting concluded, we all cheered and clapped; we returned to our work uplifted and renewed."[17]

Within a month of that gathering, Michael Yates had left the union. Others of his friends had already left and several planned to leave shortly. Chavez never flagged in exemplifying the spirit and dreams that all of them had shared to help the farmworkers; he had served as a guiding inspiration. What he had not done is prepare for the transformation of the movement into a working organization, able to maintain its commitments to the workers it served, able to function with organizational acumen, smart planning, and fiscal savvy.

Always a dogged worker himself, Chavez never was able to take the reins of power and share the responsibility. All decisions came through him. All problems came directly to his attention. Even Chavez's skilled negotiators could not make binding agreements on even routine affairs without first securing the personal approval of Chavez. Communication within the organization was poor, with Chavez's assistants were often in the dark about plans and activities.

In any autocratic regime, whether a government, a business, or a union, one individual's personal dominion over the entire leadership group is often abused through mistakes, arrogance, or ill-tempered decisions. When the Proposition 14 initiative failed, an incensed Chavez told a number of his lieutenants not to return. He became increasingly wary of the infiltration of the union by outsiders bent on doing harm. Some of his decisions relating to his staff began to appear to be based on whim and fancy and not on facts. The daily grind of responsibility weighed on Chavez, took an emotional toll, and wearied his assistants, many of whom nearly worshipped him as a folk hero.

Because of his insular governing style, Chavez feared, above all else, possible betrayal. His close working circle became tighter, with loyalty the overriding qualification. For most of the individuals who decided to leave the organization, it was never a matter of their commitment or their goal or the near unanimous respect Chavez had earned through his vision and accomplishment. It was the daily slights suffered, the sometimes-chaotic decision-making process, and the air of unrelieved tension surrounding the movement.

Michael Yates, who left La Paz to begin a teaching career, believed that the overriding difficulty with the Chavez organization was that because it was never intended to be simply a trade union but was at its core a social movement, it could not function well organizationally. Yates wrote in 1977, "I am pessimistic about the future of the UFW and the movement for it has been the vehicle to date. I fear that at present neither could survive without Chavez; they are too much dominated by his overwhelming personality."[18]

THE GREAT LETTUCE STRIKE OF 1979

Despite its administrative deficiencies and internal struggles, the UFW made substantial gains following the passage of the 1975 Agricultural Labor Relations Act. In 1978 Chavez could report that the union had signed more than 100 contracts with growers. In addition, active negotiations were in progress at another 100 ranches. "Since it was founded nearly sixteen years ago," Chavez wrote, "the union has achieved some success in raising wages and improving working conditions for farm workers in California. More important, we have destroyed the myth of grower invincibility; farm workers are no longer afraid to stand up for their rights."[19]

In January 1979, Chavez decided to strike 11 lettuce growers in the Salinas and Imperial Valleys because their offers of wage hikes were well below what the farmworkers demanded. At the time of the negotiations, lettuce pickers were making a base wage of $3.70 an hour. At first, Chavez believed that they could win their demands with a relatively short walkout. He did not anticipate the virulent opposition that the strike would set off.

At first, the solidarity among the workers raised Chavez's spirit to great heights. It was a demonstration of the enormous lengths to which the organization had traveled in establishing a disciplined and forceful union. Field workers up and down the Imperial Valley acted as one united team, with strikers bolstering each other's determination and spirits. To Chavez and other union leaders, the performance of the union members in the strike was a coming of age of the organization as a professional union.

Shocked by the unity of the farmworkers, the growers, with the lettuce crops ripening in the fields, quickly turned to their only reasonable alternative source—a new flood of illegal Mexican immigrants. One of the company spokesmen, Dennis Sullivan of United Brands, told reporters, "The people we have hired are, to the best of our knowledge, documented workers."[20] The reason that Sullivan could utter that disingenuous claim is that the growers took no pains to find out the status of the workers they hired as scab labor.

The issue of illegal immigrants not only put Chavez in a prickly political position but also in a genuinely emotional quandary. He knew first hand the poverty-wracked condition of the Mexicans who crossed the U.S. border. He felt strongly that they were cultural brothers and said on numerous occasions that they should receive amnesty and full rights of citizenship once they established roots in the country. But he also knew that their exploitation by the growers was jeopardizing the progress of the union and he called for tighter enforcement against the companies bringing across thousands of Mexican workers as strikebreakers.

Chavez and his union had become became such a symbol of Mexican American culture that the lettuce strike of 1979 featured a new element— the involvement of the Ku Klux Klan. Known predominately as defenders of the white race against blacks, the Klan entered the fray to protect whites against Mexican Americans. A cross was burned in one lettuce field. Klan workers began a recruiting effort to bring white scab labor to the fields.

Growers retaliated against Chavez with an expensive advertising campaign, impugning the integrity of Chavez himself and accusing the union of bilking workers of their wages. One school district even allowed high school students to miss classroom time so they could go to the fields to pick the lettuce crop.

On February 10, the strike turned deadly. Rufino Contreras, a 28-year-old lettuce worker, was shot dead by ranch guards. Three men were arrested on suspicion of the murder and brought before the Superior Court. Their lawyer was the law partner of the judge's son. Not surprisingly, after a few questions the prisoners were released for lack of evidence. The union held a large funeral march. The procession was led by Cesar and Helen Chavez and attended by Governor Brown.

The violence continued in the fields. Police lobbed tear gas canisters into bands of strikers on a number of occasions. When some of the strikers lobbed the canisters back at the police they were hauled off to the police station. A number of fights broke out. When asked to comment on the violence, Chavez pointed out that all of the bloodshed in the confrontations appeared to come only from the union members.

In late summer of 1979, Chavez called for a march on Salinas. It lasted 12 days with two groups parading from San Francisco, more 100 miles to the north, and from San Ardo, 70 miles to the south. With Chavez in the northern contingent were 6 horsemen and 22 mariachi musicians in the lead and union workers carrying red banners. More than 25,000 individuals took part in the march. Union leaders welcomed the sight of workers in the fields who threw down their tools and joined the march when it passed.

When the marchers from San Francisco reached Salinas, Chavez, who had fasted for part of the journey, looked pale. Nevertheless, when the marchers reached the center of town, merged with the other farmworkers and filled the center of town, Chavez smiled broadly.

At Salinas's Hartnell Community College gymnasium, the farmworkers held a rally attended by many state politicians, including Brown. As they prepared to leave the gym, Chavez rose and ordered them to stop. "Fasten your seatbelts," he smiled. "There is an important announcement to come."[21]

It was the signing of a contract with Meyer Tomato Company, a leading tomato grower. The contract provided a raise in wages from $4.50 an hour to $5.15 and guarantees that senior workers will not be replaced by machines. Chavez beamed. More victories, he sensed, were on the way.

NOTES

1. Edmund G. Brown Jr., "Chavez Based His Life on Sharing and Frugality," *San Francisco Examiner*, 25 April 1993, p. 2

2. "10,000 in Protest At Gallo Winery," *New York Times*, 2 March 1975, p. 44.

3. Jacques Levy, *Cesar Chavez: Autobiography of La Causa,* http://chavez. cde.ca.gov/ModelCurriculum/Teachers/Lessons/Resources/Documents/Chavez_ Biography_by_Levy.PDF.

4. Studs Terkel, *Working.* (New York: Avon Books, 1974), p. 34–37.

5. Susan Ferriss and Ricardo Sandoval, "The Death of the Short-Handled Hoe," http://www.pbs.org/itvs/fightfields/book1.html.

6. Marjorie Cohn, "The Death of El Cortito," http://www.truthout.org/ docs_2005/L012505A.shtml.

7. "Latino Attorney Honored by Farm Workers' Rights Group," 21 November, 2001, http://www.laprensasandiego.org/archieve/november21/lawyer.htm.

8. Susan Ferriss and Ricardo Sandoval.

9. Ibid.

10. Anita Quintanilla, "Remembering a Modest Cesar," http://www.azteca. net/aztec/modest_cesar.html.

11. Edmund G. Brown Jr.

12. Anita Quintanilla.

13. Father Ken Irrgang, "Cesar Chavez: A Spiritual Man," http://www. the-tidings.com/2004/0402/cesar.htm.

14. Ibid.

15. Vernal Seagraves, "Cesar Chavez and the Farm Workers: Victories, Yes, but the Struggle Goes On," *The Christian Century* (17 December 1975), 1161.

16. "Cesar's Triumph," *Newsweek* (21 March 1977), 72.

17. Michael Yates, "A Union Is Not a 'Movement,'" *The Nation* (19 November 1977), 518.

18. Ibid.

19. Cesar Chavez, "The Farm Workers Next Battle, *The Nation* (25 March 1978), 332.

20. "A Lettuce Strike Takes Unusual Turn," *U.S. News & World Report* (28 May 1979), 60.

21. "Chavez Says UFW Strike Will Spread," *World* (19 August 1979), http:// www.sfsu.edu/~cecipp/cesar_chavez/ufwstrike.htm.

Chapter 9

VIVA LA CAUSA

When Cesar Chavez looked back over the two decades of the farmworkers' movement, he saw the landscape far differently than he did when he first moved with his wife and children to Delano with little more than hopes and determination. In the early days of the movement, it was difficult to get anyone in the fields to talk about a union. The men and women were afraid, intimidated, stifled in a system and a way of life that seemed overwhelming and impossible to change.

Chavez's movement, with its energy and appeal to the religious and cultural heritage of Mexican Americans, had lit a spark in the harvest fields that consumed old notions that life could not improve, that the system holding down the workers was too intractable and too powerful to be changed. Through grit and stubbornness, Chavez and his lieutenants had whacked away at the stereotypes and the defeatism and convinced large numbers of people that they could fight back.

To those who claimed that the organization was not a labor union; to those who claimed that his tactics and direction were something alien to the typical labor-management relationship; and to those who claimed that his alliance was a strange mixture of cultural, religious, and political ingredients, he agreed: "Those who attack our union often say it's not really a union," Chavez said,

> It's something else, a social movement, a civil rights movement, it's something dangerous. They're half right. The United Farm Workers is first and foremost a union, a union like any other, a union that either produces for its members on the bread-and-butter issues or doesn't

survive. But the UFW has always been something more than a union, although it's never been dangerous, if you believe in the Bill of Rights. The UFW was the beginning. We attacked that historical source of shame and infamy that our people in this country lived with. We attacked that injustice, not by complaining, not by seeking handouts, not by becoming soldiers in the war on poverty; we organized.[1]

Even Chavez's harshest critics, California's growers, acknowledged that the organizing movement on behalf of the farmworkers had produced very tangible benefits. In the mid-1960s, farmworkers earned an average of less than $2 an hour; two decades later, they earned over $5.00 an hour.

Chavez talked about consolidating those gains and the overriding need to keep members involved in union activities. He talked about the need to train and energize younger members, and to realize that the struggle for the rights of farmworkers had only begun. When the union was flush with new contracts with growers after the Agricultural Labor Relations Act and when the political winds were with the farmworkers under the Brown administration in Sacramento, Chavez feared that the men and women who had fought so hard would tend to feel that the battles through which they had just emerged were the decisive ones, that the threat was over and the war was won. He sensed that the new contracts and higher wages would lead to complacency and that the spirit of reform that energized the movement in the first place would suffer.

His own responsibility, Chavez believed, was to keep up the momentum and to keep the union ready for the tougher times ahead. Even with the extraordinary accomplishments thus far, the farmworkers remained on the lower rung of labor's ladder. They needed health care, job security, decent living conditions, access to education programs, and a semblance of economic security. The union, Chavez believed, should be there for them even when, at times, they might not be there for the union.

He was determined to keep moving forward and to keep a strong leadership role. Chavez said on a number of occasions that he had given up most of his private life for the union. Helen and his children could testify to that assertion. Almost all of their relationships with Chavez centered on union activities. They had to suffer long absences from Chavez, not only when he was on the road but at La Paz, where he often remained isolated with his associates.

The dissension within the ranks of the union reached new and dangerous levels in the early 1980s. A number of Chavez's closest supporters over the years drifted off to other jobs and other interests. Marshall Ganz, one of Chavez's ablest organizers, reluctantly left the job for an academic life. The union's lead attorney, Jerry Cohen, and Chavez's close friend, Gilbert Padilla, also departed. A number of Chavez's assistants were dismissed when they openly attacked the administration of the union. Chavez, they insisted, was an enormously successful crusader for justice but a less than adequate administrator. Many pointed to the enormous backlog in the union's medical plan, where claims were being processed at a glacier's pace.

Chavez's domineering leadership of the union had reached new levels, according to some. Philip Vera Cruz, a 20-year veteran in the grape fields who was at one time a vice president of the union, later said, "One thing the union would never allow was for people to criticize Cesar. If a union leader is built up as a symbol and he talks like he was God, then there is no way you can have true democracy in the union because the members are just generally deprived of their right to reason for themselves."[2] Chavez wanted more than some of the members felt they could give. He demanded tight control over the organization he founded. He wanted nonstop crusaders.

A REPUBLICAN IN SACRAMENTO

In November 1982, Los Angeles Mayor Tom Bradley became the first black person nominated by a major party to run for a governorship. Bradley had long admired Chavez. Unhappily for Chavez and the UFW, Bradley narrowly lost the election to Republican George Deukmejian.

Born in Menands, New York, Deukmejian was the son of Armenian immigrants from Iran. Veteran state legislator and state attorney general, Deukmejian was not an ultraconservative in the mold of Ronald Reagan. Nevertheless, he amassed strong support from California's agribusiness community. The growers contributed over one million dollars to his campaign. With Deukmejian now stepping into the executive mansion in Sacramento replacing Jerry Brown, the UFW had been handed a whole new deck of legislative cards. There would likely be no winning hands.

Deukmejian did not disappoint the growers. He packed the Agricultural Labor Relations Board with representatives who supported the interests of the growers. The new general counsel of the board, for example, was a long-time California politician who believed that the state, in its dealings with the farmworkers, had gone too far in jeopardizing the agricultural industry. Under the new leadership of the board, enforcement of the farm labor election law became gnarled in delay and inaction. Chavez's union thus had no state authority to which it could issue appeals of grower labor violations and expect action.

Roberto De La Cruz, director of the UFW's field offices in the Salinas Valley, told a *New York Times* reporter that Deukmejian was "telling the growers that they can do anything they can get away with."[3]

Nevertheless, despite the efforts of Deukmejian and his allies in the California legislature, the Agricultural Labor Relations Act was never rescinded during the two four-year terms of the governor. Indeed, the law was never even amended, much to the chagrin of growers who sought to reduce its scope and authority. Deukmejian was able to reduce the law's impact while he was in office but was not able to kill or wound its authority.

Much of the resilience of the law can be traced to the political savvy that Chavez had acquired as head of the union. Despite the opposition of a number of his associates, Chavez began to use some of the very limited funds of the union to support Democratic candidates for the California legislature.

One of the key figures that Chavez courted with his support was the new speaker of the assembly, Willie Brown. With Chavez's persistent lobbying campaign of Brown and others in the legislature, the labor law's supporters fended off numerous attempts to dismantle the legislation that Chavez had worked so hard to secure a decade earlier. Nevertheless, despite its failure to change the farm labor law, George Deukmejian tried as hard as he could to make life miserable for Chavez and his union.

Growers soon realized that if they simply ignored the farmworkers' law during the Deukmejian administration, they would not be prosecuted. Even on some of the farms that had held elections and had chosen the UFW as their union, the process came to a grinding halt with the Republicans in control in Sacramento. For example, workers at D'Arrigo Brothers, a big Salinas Valley grower that produces broccoli and other vegetables, had voted to unionize in 1975 and still did not have a formal contract nearly a decade later.

In speeches around the state, Chavez denounced Deukmejian. Since he took office, Chavez told an audience in San Francisco, Deukmejian had paid back his debt to agribusiness with the blood and sweat of the farmworkers. What did Deukmejian's governorship mean for the farmworkers, Chavez asked? "It means that the right to vote in free elections is a sham. It means the right to talk freely about the union among your fellow workers on the job is a cruel hoax. It means that the right to be free from threats and intimidation by growers is an empty promise. It means that the right to sit down and negotiate with your employer as equals across the bargaining table and not as peons in the fields is a fraud."[4]

Chavez felt increasing pressures and skepticism as he sought to find the most effective strategies to carry on the fight. Newspapers and magazines began once again to report that the union's membership, as well as its power, was in decline. He fended off political attacks that his own managing style was contributing to a declining loyalty and camaraderie among the farm workers.

Chavez admitted the lower numbers but insisted that the influence of the union extended beyond the current membership. He pointed out that the very fact of the union's existence forced an entire entrenched industry to spend millions of dollars yearly in responding to the issues of fair pay and benefits for workers, issues raised by the union in their marches and boycotts. If the union were as weak as the critics claimed, Chavez asked, why did the agribusiness interests spend such large amounts of money to fight it? The actual number of members of the union at any one time was not the main point, Chavez claimed. The fact was that hundreds of thousands of farm workers in California and other states were better off since the advent of the farmworkers' union, even if they did not personally work under a union contract. The work of the union was all about pride and dignity of the farmworkers who were taking control of their own lives.

The most serious accusations about the union appeared in an article authored by the nationally syndicated muckraking reporter Jack Anderson. A winner of the Pulitzer Prize, Anderson's columns were read avidly across the nation by millions.

Without any warning, Anderson suddenly went on the offensive against Chavez, a surprising turn considering the fact that the journalist had always seemed to be a Chavez admirer. Anderson talked in harsh terms of the current state of the UFW—that it was raising large amounts of money from celebrities and was not using it for the union; that it was becoming a tyrannical organization under a leader who was increasingly enamored of power; and, finally, that it was even encouraging violence.

To back up the claim about violence, Anderson cited the case of an investigative reporter who was supposedly attacked and beaten by union supporters in Arizona while Chavez stood by and watched. It was a breathtaking charge—that Chavez, the leader whom some were comparing to Gandhi, would encourage his own supporters to violence.

Stunned and infuriated by the accusation, Chavez decided to fight the allegations with the best lawyer he could find. He hired Melvin Belli. Soon, the famed lawyer had Anderson and others involved in the story in fast retreat. The reported beating, it soon became clear, had never occurred. The individual who was supposed to have endured the assault admitted that the story was untrue. Others in the audience on the night of the supposed beating testified that no such beating occurred. Anderson himself visited La Paz, where a team of union lawyers showed him and others the financial records that showed where the contributions had been spent. Anderson publicly retracted the story against Chavez, a remarkable admission from the famous journalist. Anderson also revealed that the source of much he had reported had been consultants hired by right-wing publishing interests and wealthy agribusiness representatives.

Chavez had labored his entire career to practice and encourage nonviolence. Throughout its life, the farmworkers' movement had been notable for the restraint shown by its followers. In 1983, that restraint would again be tested.

THE SHOOTING OF RENE LOPEZ

On September 21, 1983, at the Sikkema Dairy Farm near Fresno, California, farmworker Rene Lopez, a 19-year-old native of Nuevo León, Mexico, was shot to death. There was violence on the picket lines of California, Chavez had said many times, and almost all of it was directed at farmworkers. Lopez's death again fired the determination of union workers and of Chavez himself to bring to the attention of the nation the injustices of the agribusiness interests and their enforcers.

Lopez had moved with his family to the San Joaquin Valley in 1974. Quiet and intelligent, he graduated from Carruthers High School, fluent in both Spanish and English. When he joined a number of his friends as a field laborer at the dairy farm, he was asked by his fellow campesinos to become their spokesperson. They were anxious to join the UFW and asked Lopez to take the lead in negotiating their interests.

When he was still in high school, Lopez became interested in the union. He traveled to Stockton to support a farmworkers' strike and to learn more about union activities. He was thrilled to be asked by the workers at the dairy to become their spokesperson.

When Lopez informed grower Fred Sikkema that the workers intended to join the farmworkers' union and that they intended to ask for an increase in wages, the dairy farmer was furious. He warned Lopez that he would fire those who joined the union and would force the remaining workers to put in even longer hours.

Lopez was not intimidated by Sikkema's threats. He and several other workers at the dairy met with UFW organizers to plan the next steps in joining the union. Roberto Escutia, of the farmworkers' Horticulture Division, was assigned to help Lopez in filing for a union representation election at the Sikkema Dairy. In the meantime, the workers decided to strike the dairy.

The picket lines at the dairy entrance threw Sikkema into a rage. He hired several thugs to try to break up the gathering. During the first days of the election campaign, Dolores Lopez, Rene's mother, said that her son came home one evening proudly saying, "Today I am a man. Today I signed a UFW authorization card to become a member of the United Farm Workers."[5]

A few days later, two of the enforcers drove past the workers on their way to meet Sikkema in one of the dairy buildings. After meeting with the dairyman, they drove back to the workers and motioned to Lopez to approach the car. As he walked over to the passenger side of the car to within about three feet, one of the men pulled a gun and shot Lopez through the head.

Hundreds of farm workers joined the Lopez family in Fresno. They brought with them flower baskets and wreaths with the names of unions from all over California. One small wreath was from Lopez's fiancée. It said *Querido Novio* ("Beloved Sweetheart"). The two were supposed to have been married the weekend he was murdered.

At the funeral, Chavez told the mourners,

How many more farm workers must fall? How many more tears must be shed? How many more martyrs must there be before we can be free? When will the day come when the joy becomes great and the grief becomes small? The answer, my brothers and sisters, is in our hands. The answer is in *our* hands. We who live must now walk an extra mile because Rene has lived and died for *his* and *our* dreams. We who keep on struggling for justice for farm workers must carry in our hearts *his* sacrifice. We must try to live as he lived ... We must keep alive his hopes ... and fulfill, with our own sacrifices, his dreams. We must take Rene into our hearts and promise that we will never forget his sacrifice.[6]

In the ensuing trial of the gunmen, one was found guilty of manslaughter and sentenced to seven years in prison. The other was acquitted. Fred Sikkema was not charged by the District Attorney for any part in the killing.

There had been earlier killings of farmworkers on the picket lines in the life of the farm union. This one touched Chavez especially hard. Much of the blame he attributed to the Deukmejian administration in Sacramento and the clear signals it had spread throughout the agribusiness community that violations of the farmworkers' law would not be prosecuted. If it had not been for the drastic budget cuts and changes in personnel of the Agricultural Labor Relations Board, Rene Lopez and the other workers at the Sikkema Dairy would have had beside them a group of government overseers to ensure that the election proceeded fairly. As it was, no representative from the board had been at the dairy. The way had been cleared for tragedy.

Chavez was especially worried that, with this new outrage, it would be difficult to keep in check the workers' natural instincts for retaliation. How many more times could he make them believe that nonviolence would triumph? He still knew he was on the right road but also knew that it was as dangerous and treacherous as ever.

In a full counteroffensive, Chavez set out once again to prove the critics and naysayers wrong. He went back to a trusted weapon—the boycott.

A NEW BOYCOTT

In 1984, Chavez called for another grape boycott. He talked about the exploitation of the farmworkers by the growers. "For generations," he said, "they have subjugated entire races of dark-skinned farm workers. These are the sins of growers, not the farm workers. We didn't poison the land, we didn't open the door to imported produce, we didn't covet billions of dollars in government handouts, we didn't abuse and exploit the people who work the land. Today the growers are like a punch-drunk old boxer who doesn't know he's past his prime. The times are changing; the political and social environment has changed. The chickens are coming home to roost, and the time to account for past sins is approaching."[7]

In a fiery speech in Fresno, Chavez told supporters that Deukmejian's efforts to undermine the Agricultural Labor Relations Act and to bury the UFW were a new call to action. He declared, "Let us take off where we left off in 1975 with the most effective weapon which served us so well—the consumer boycott—and see how they like it."[8]

Chavez scoffed at the critics who talked about the discouragement and pessimism of the farmworkers' movement. He talked about the Republican political control of the state and the White House and the conservative direction in which the country seemed to be moving. The farmworkers would take on the challenges with the same energy and drive that had marked the beginnings of their fight for workers' rights. The future was on the side of the workers, he said. They and their children and other Hispanics in California and other states, driven by the cultural passion and spirit of reform set by the farmworkers' movement, would inevitably take power from the corporate forces. They would do it with a force of numbers and with a burning will to overcome.

When he looked down the road two or three decades, he said, he saw communities such as Modesto, Salinas, and Bakersfield as well as the great cities of the California dominated by the economic power and the votes of the children of farmworkers, not the children of the big growers. The new grape strike he announced would drive home to millions of Americans the continuing need to reform the harvest fields of California and the farm labor areas in the rest of the United States.

As if to highlight his announcement of a new strike, the press picked up on a story that demonstrated in the most graphic detail the humiliating and degrading existence that workers in twentieth-century America still endured. The story was from a 300-acre strawberry farm near Salinas, California. It was owned by 59-year-old Jose Ballin.

In the fall of 1985, Ballin and his ranch were suddenly overrun by uninvited guests: television news cameras, print reporters, and California government officials who had been tipped off about the conditions under which Ballin made his field workers live. Mostly undocumented workers from Mexico, the field hands basically lived in dark holes they had cut into a steep hill on the ranch. The little caves were just large enough for the body of one worker. Others slept in old tractors; some had constructed makeshift hovels pasted together with sticks and cardboard.

The questioning of the farm owner made the jaws of some of the most seasoned reporters drop. Ballin was actually charging each worker twenty-five cents an hour for rental of the holes they had dug in the ground or for space in the tractors and hovels in which they slept. Newly hired workers were given a shovel and told "to dig themselves a home." The only available water for the workers was an irrigation pipe. They used a eucalyptus grove as a toilet.[9]

This was not a scene out of a poverty-wracked third world country or one of photographer Dorothea Lange's black and white photographs from the most wretched scenes of the Great Depression. This was a lush, verdant valley of California in 1985.

In magazine, newspaper, and television coverage, reporters began to call the place "Rancho las Cuevas" (Ranch of the Caves). Some of the stories showed pictures of one of the laborers crawling on all fours in and out of his tiny space. On the sides of the cave, he had pinned small pictures of the religious saints and some letters from his family in Mexico.

This, Chavez said, is what the farmworkers' struggle was all about, this fight for social justice, this crusade to make humane an inhumane system and to give back to individuals the basic rights that are humanly theirs. The movement, he said, was a profound way to say yes to human dignity.

With the new boycott, Chavez began to change his tactics with the times. "I told Cesar the old days of Xeroxed leaflets were over," said Richard Ross, the son of Chavez's close friend Fred Ross. "The kids that used to march in parades against the Vietnam War are now driving BMW's and going out for Sunday brunch. You've got to do something different."[10]

Although Chavez still intended to involve mostly the farmworkers in the new boycott, many of whom drove nothing at all, let alone BMWs, he did listen to Ross's advice. This would be a new, high technology campaign. They would fight the growers not only with their marches but also with new computers and with demographic studies to select people most likely to support a boycott. They would use the latest advertising methods to attempt to change buying habits and to alter the image of certain store chains that had rebuffed the union's pleas.

The union purchased a Sperry mainframe computer. By sorting through census and voting records and employment information, the union targeted Hispanics, liberal professionals, and middle-class blacks in such cities as New York, San Francisco, and Los Angeles. To these people, the union sent over two million computerized letters, explaining why they had called for a boycott and asking for support. "We need to innovate and take risks with new ways of doing things or we'll go out of business," Chavez said. "Way deep inside me there is something about computers I don't like. I seldom go into the computer room. But the other side has them, and we need to compete."[11]

Richard Ross could not have said it better. Chavez hoped to stir an entirely new generation of Americans who matured politically and socially in the 1960s and 1970s with something approaching the intensity with which he had stirred supporters two decades earlier. He wanted a new generation to see the boycott as a socially accepted behavior, just as students on college campuses and young, liberal professional people had seen it at an earlier time.

By the end of 1984, Chavez reported encouraging progress. He told his listeners that the union must translate the importance of the farmworkers' movement into the language of the 1980s. "They are responding not to picket lines and leafleting alone, but to the high-tech boycott of today, a boycott that uses computers and direct mail and advertising techniques, which has revolutionized business and politics in recent years. We have achieved more success with a boycott in the first 11 months of 1984 than we achieved in the last 14 years, since 1970."[12]

CRUSADING AGAINST PESTICIDE POISONING

In 1985, in the middle of the grape boycott, Chavez decided to increase the pressures on the growers in another controversial area—the use of pesticides. He announced that, as part of the boycott, the union would launch a campaign entitled "Wrath of Grapes." The union had used the title for a short documentary film it had produced a few years earlier demonstrating evidence of birth defects and high cancer rates among the children of farm workers caused by the use of pesticides in the southern San Joaquin Valley. Now was the time, Chavez felt, for a full-scale war on pesticide poisoning.

The pesticides, some of which were applied by airplanes, routinely drifted away from targeted fields and landed on workers and their families and easily reached their living quarters. Even when the spray accurately hit the targeted area, small amounts of the chemicals remained on the plants. When workers who thinned and harvested crops reentered the fields after the spraying, they inhaled the chemicals and touched and rubbed them into their eyes. Studies had begun to suggest that farmworkers and their children were vulnerable to a long list of illnesses potentially related to pesticides, including not only cancer and birth defects, but also liver disease, childhood leukemia, and infertility.

Chavez talked about the cumulative effect that pesticides, herbicides, soil fumigants, and fertilizers had produced in the soil and water. Thousands of acres in California alone, he claimed, had been irrevocably contaminated by the unrestrained, wanton use of these chemicals. Many thousands more, he said, would be lost unless growers were prevented from dumping an ever-increasing amount.

He talked about the hundreds of consumer illnesses in 1985 that resulted from irresponsible use of the insecticide Aldicarb on watermelons. He talked about how the health authorities in many San Joaquin Valley towns had already warned young children and pregnant mothers not to drink the water, because of the nitrates from fertilizers which had poisoned the ground water. He talked about such poisons as Captan, Parathion, Phosdrin, and methyl bromide covering the plants and the workers who harvest them. "People should demand grapes free of pesticide," he said. "People buying California table grapes are being poisoned."[13]

Ed Begley Jr., the son of Hollywood actor Ed Begley, grew up in Van Nuys, California, and, as a teenager followed Chavez's career with much admiration. In 1985, Begley ran into Chavez by accident. "I was at a coffee shop on Sepulveda having a bowl of oatmeal and a guy pulled up in a car with another," Begley said. "I thought that guy looks a lot like Cesar Chavez, but I knew it couldn't be him. It was a tiny little car. There was only one guy, no entourage. There was no security team that any labor leader of the time would have had. This was a guy like Jimmy Hoffa, a big labor leader. But when he walked by, there was no mistake. It was Cesar Chavez. I walked up to him and asked him if the grape boycott was still on. He said, 'Yes, because of the pesticides'. I offered to help and he said, 'Give me your number.'"[14] Begley began working with Chavez and the United Farm Workers on the issue, not only donating time and money but also helping organize the Hollywood political community behind the cause.

Consumer advocate Ralph Nader also joined Chavez in the boycott. Nader encouraged "all consumers to boycott fresh table grapes both for their own health and to send a clear message to growers, chemical companies, grocery retailers, and government officials that the reckless use of deadly poisons which threatens the health of farm workers and consumers will no longer be tolerated."[15] At the same time Nader championed Chavez's boycott of grapes, his own organization released a study about a pesticide called Alar that was used extensively on apples. The study claimed that Alar caused cancer in children.

The boycott focused on five pesticides that had been listed as possibly hazardous by the Environmental Protection Agency (EPA). A spokesperson for the agency, in response to the boycott, said that all five, if used without special precautions, could be potentially dangerous. In those three words—"without special precautions"—was the crux of the argument between those who supported the boycott and the growers.

As with any claims of cause and effect on health by chemicals, the two sides produced their own studies and their own scientists to prove entirely opposite conclusions. In response to the UFW's claims about the effects of specific poisons, Bruce Obbink, 53, president of the California Table Grape Commission, became something of the public face of the growers. National magazines and newspapers reported his charges that Chavez was duping the American public on the issue of pesticides. "I'm not interested in discrediting him," Obbink said. "Cesar Chavez has done a lot of good work for the farm worker. If it weren't for Chavez, there would not be this farm labor law in place. It's his law. There would not be a unionization effort. But, he's lost sight of what he's supposed to be doing, and that is organizing farm workers." There was absolutely no evidence, Obbink said, that the pesticide levels were dangerous either to the health of farmworkers and consumers or to the soil and water supplies.[16]

Governor Deukmejian accused Chavez and his supporters of making "false and irresponsible" charges that pesticides used on California table grapes pose a health hazard to consumers, field workers and the environment. "It is unfair and irresponsible for a handful of political and entertainment celebrities to malign the solid international reputation of our farm products, when they have absolutely no evidence to back up their outrageous charges," the governor said during his weekly radio address. "I want to assure consumers that California grapes are safe and wholesome, and that the charges made by the boycott sponsors are false and irresponsible."[17]

Asked for comment on Deukmejian's radio speech, a UFW spokesperson, Chris Hartmire, said:

The governor was elected with millions of dollars from agribusiness. He always has been a spokesperson for agribusiness. But the grape growers really must be feeling the pressure of the boycott or the governor would not be stooping to doing free radio ads for them. It's kind of sad for the governor of all the people to choose to use his air time on behalf of one wealthy and backward industry when the health of all Californians is at stake.[18]

Chavez took his crusade against unsafe pesticide use around the United States, visiting various cities to give speeches and conduct meeting. In the summer of 1988, back in his headquarters at Delano, he began a fast.

He was now 61 years old. Helen Chavez, other family members and friends, as well as Chavez's doctors, were very concerned that he would again jeopardize his health. When he began the fast, he described it as an act of "personal purification" as well as a call for action, a "declaration of non-cooperation" with stores that sold table grapes, and "penance for those who could do more."[19]

As Chavez's fast extended over a month, his health deteriorated to the extent that doctors began to fear for his life. Helen, who had remained extremely worried throughout the entire month, was controlled in public but privately fearful that she might lose her husband within a matter of days. His daughter Linda remembered it as one of the most frightening times of her life. Even former colleagues such as Marshall Ganz and Jerry Cohen who had left the UFW returned to implore Chavez to end the fast.

Finally, after 36 days, he agreed. On August 21, 1988, two of Chavez's sons carried the union leader into a large tent. Flanked by Helen and his 96-year-old mother, Juana, Chavez, sitting in a rocking chair, accepted a piece of bread from Ethel Kennedy.

Months after he had regained his strength after the fast, Chavez was back on the campaign. In Washington State he told students at Pacific Lutheran College that the UFW would never back off its pressure at all levels of government on the issue of pesticide poisoning. From those who picked the crops to those who consumed them, there was no more important issue, he said, than the safety of their lives.

In late 2003, long after Chavez's boycott and fast, a farmworker named Juan Rios talked to a reporter in the Sunnyside, Washington, office of the UFW. On the wall above him is a portrait of Chavez. Rios talked of the serious effects on his own health that pesticides caused when he had been asked to do some of the spraying. "I went to the doctor, but he didn't give me anything," Rios says. "He just told me to stop working with the pesticides."[20]

In the years since Chavez's strong advocacy of protection against pesticides, the problem still simmers. The UFW's claims about the effects of pesticides took on a significant stamp of legitimacy when the National Academy of Sciences proposed that the agriculture industry in the United States gradually eliminate the use of pesticides in favor of natural cultivation.

On September 11, 1989, five supermarket chains in the United States and Canada said they would ask food suppliers to disclose pesticides used on their crops and ask them to phase out use of 64 carcinogenic pesticides.

Yet, into the twenty-first century, of the 2.5 million farm workers nationwide, 300,000 are poisoned to some degree each year, according to estimates by the EPA; 800 to 1,000 of those individuals die, says a report of the U.S. Bureau of Labor Statistics. Although EPA actions have resulted in the removal of some of the most dangerous pesticides from the market, environmental activists continue to press for additional reform.[21]

The National Cancer Institute and the National Institute for Occupational Safety and Health are conducting large studies measuring pesticide exposure and related illness in farmworkers, but the final results are not due for over a decade. Only one state collects detailed information about the types and amounts of pesticides used in the fields—California, where the UFW continues its fight for occupational safety, a crusade that had been of vital importance to its founder, Cesar Chavez.

NOTES

1. Cesar Chavez, "What the Future Holds for Farm Workers and Hispanics," Speech at the Commonwealth Club, San Francisco, http://www.mindfully.org/Reform/Cesar-Chavez9nov84.htm.

2. Frank Bardacke, "Cesar's Ghost," *The Nation* (26 July 1993), 133.

3. "Pioneer Farm Labor Act Is Imperiled in California," *New York Times*, 22 May 1983, 24.

4. Chavez, "What the Future Holds."

5. "Rene Lopez (1962–1983)," http://www.clnet.ucla.edu/research/chavez/themes/ufw/rene.htm.

6. Ibid.

7. Chavez, "What the Future Holds."

8. "Cesar Chavez Tries New Directions for United Farm Workers," *New York Times*, 19 September 1983, 16.

9. Miriam Wells, *Strawberry Fields: Politics, Class and Work in California Agriculture* (Ithaca: Cornell University Press, 1996), 211.

10. "Chavez and Farm Workers Adapt Tactics to the Times," *New York Times*, 31 July 1983, 20.

11. "Chavez Tries a Computerized Grape Boycott," *Business Week*, 9 September 1985, 36.

12. Chavez, "What the Future Holds."

13. Carlos Byars, "Chavez Aims Wrath at Grapes/Labor Leader Pitches Pesticide Issue to Rally Support for Boycott," *Houston Chronicle*, September 24, 1986, 29.

14. Jeffrey St. Clair, "Render unto Cesar: Songs and Dances from the Fields of Pain," *Dissident Voice*, 12 April 2003, http://www.dissidentvoice.org/Articles4/StClair_Chavez.htm.

15. "Boycott of Table Grapes by Union is Backed," *New York Times*, 23 December 1987, 10.

16. Barbara Reynolds, "Grape Boycott is a Hoax on the Public," *USA Today*, 21 July 1987, 11.

17. Jerry Gillam, "Deukmejian Accuses Chavez, Backers of 'Irresponsible' Charges on Grapes," *Los Angeles Times*, 28 August 1988, 30.

18. Ibid.

19. "Fast by Chavez Over Pesticides Passes 29th Day," *New York Times*, 16 August 1988, 18.

20. Rebecca Clarren, "Harvesting Poison," 29 September 2003, http://www.headwatersnews.org/HCN.farmworkers.html.

21. Jerome Blondell, "Epidemiology of Pesticide Poisonings in the United States," *Occupational Medicine: State of the Art Reviews*, 1997, 209–220.

Chapter 10

THE REACH OF THE REFORMER

"I was 14 when I helped to organize the grape and lettuce boycotts in Indianapolis," Jeffrey St. Clair recalled.

> We were not an overwhelming force by any means. There were five or six of us at most meetings. We targeted a different store each weekend. On my first picket, I parked myself in front of a Kroger's on the south side of Indianapolis—the albino suburb of a city that's whiter than Carrera marble. I harangued housewives about the conditions of farm workers on their way in and on the way out. They looked at me as if I was a lunatic, horrified at the prospect that I was one of their neighbor's children. Would one of their own come home one day in the grip of a similar fever? They had good cause to think I'd gone around the bend.[1]

On one occasion, the 14-year-old so exhausted the patience of the shoppers at the Kroger's supermarket that the management resorted to calling the sheriff. When the lawman told Jeffrey to leave, he refused. Off to jail he went with the sheriff, who locked the boy in a bathroom so that he would not have to spend time behind real bars. As he recalled later, "It was my first arrest. There would be others in the months and years ahead. The usual story of an obnoxious child. Thank you, Cesar Chavez for giving me my start in a life of political crime."[2]

When St. Clair began his youthful protest, he had never met or seen a migrant worker. He had only one Hispanic friend. Nevertheless, when he heard Chavez speak in Indianapolis after the assassinations of Martin

Luther King Jr. and Robert Kennedy, he became a fan. He followed in the newspapers Chavez's fast, he said, like someone following a soap opera. Although St. Clair did not work with Chavez, he did become an award-winning investigative journalist, author, and environmental activist, arguing forcefully for many of the ideas advanced by Chavez.

Across the country and through the years, Chavez had a mesmerizing effect on the lives of thousands. They saw in him nobility, sacrifice, and the grit of the underdog that refuses to give up.

Tomás Villanueva was one of those thousands. Born in Monterrey, Mexico, in 1941, Villanueva was a migrant worker in his youth in Texas, Ohio, Idaho, and Washington. Living in a labor shanty camp north of Toppenish, Washington, he and other members of his family worked cutting asparagus for the California Packing Company. They shared a one-room cabin with bunk beds and a wood stove for cooking. They also shared one outside shower for men and one for women with 60 other workers. All the workers got their water from one faucet.

Villanueva had heard from other workers about a man called Chavez and a new labor movement for field workers in California. Villanueva and a friend traveled to Delano to try to meet Chavez.

> We expected him to be in a nice office and we end up in an old run-down neighborhood, a run-down house. There was his office. We went up in there and asked for him and he came out himself, in a real humble way, and he says, "I'm Cesar Chavez, What can I do for you boys?" Lupe and I explained, "Well, we come from the state of Washington. We heard a lot about you, but all we hear is from the news media and we'd like to hear it from you—what is with you and farm workers in the state of California?" "Well, if [you] guys want to know about what I'm doing and what we are doing here, instead of me telling you, why don't you just stay and work with me for a couple of weeks?"[3]

They did stay, sleeping on a concrete floor. The visit made a lifelong impression on Villaneuva. The most important lesson, he said, was Chavez's insistence that the farmworkers themselves must unite as a community to assert their rights. In the name of their own humanity and dignity, they must stand against their oppressive situation and those that enforced it.

He said later that Chavez's social commitment for the farm laborer held up in plain sight, in all its ugliness, the blatant racism and cultural discrimination that faced Mexican Americans. "Our children were called dumb and always dropping out of school," Villaneuva said, "Our children were being taken to the fields to cut asparagus at 4, 4:30 in the morning, leaving from home at 9 or 10 to school. I mean, they didn't want to study—they wanted to fall asleep on the desk." It was this kind of stereotype and the indignities that resulted that the Chavez movement so dramatically challenged. Villaneuva wanted to become part of it.[4]

He left Delano and returned to Washington with a much clearer mission for his own life. He helped launch the Yakima, Washington, branch of the UFW and served as its first president from 1986 to 1992.

Two years before his death, Chavez paid homage to one of his heroes. In a speech he called "Lessons of Dr. Martin Luther King, Jr.," Chavez said that many people think of King as only a civil rights leader. Not so, said Chavez. "He had a much broader agent." Chavez talked about King's tireless crusading for the poor, his forthright opposition to the Vietnam war based on his religious convictions and his belief in nonviolence, and his fights for the rights of workers and their children. He pointed out that King was in Memphis at the time of his assassination on behalf of sanitation workers. "Dr. King's dedication to the rights of the workers who are so often exploited by the forces of greed has profoundly touched my life and guided my struggle," Chavez said.[5]

In the same way that Chavez encouraged others to think of King as much more than a civil rights leader, it is important to see Chavez as more than an individual who simply began a labor union.

When Chavez reflected on his own life and on the influences that drove him to his work, he saw in his past a brew of anger, rage, and humiliation. His motivation, he said, came from watching the struggles of his mother and father and from his own experiences with life in the fields and the instances in which the system was fixed so that an individual was made to feel more like a farm implement than a human. It was from watching family and friends treated as if they were disposable chattel, like cows and horses. It was from watching abuse doled out by the few against the many and the feeling that such exploitation must be challenged.

As he grew older, he said, he began to think of the struggles of the farmworkers in larger terms, as the shared struggles of all Mexican Americans. All, he said, were connected to the experience of the farmworkers, whether in the United States or Mexico. All shared common humiliations and shattered pride. How could Hispanics progress as a people, he asked, if the farmworkers, whose lives were shared by the parents or grandparents of a large percentage of the Hispanic population, were denied self-respect?

As with other cultural and racial minorities, he wrote, the answer was in organizing. More Mexican Americans had to educate themselves to wield increasing economic and political power and had to coalesce around common dreams and aspirations. The beginnings of a social movement lie in burdens shared and goals reached together.

Many Hispanics in cities and towns across the country closely identified with the struggle of the farmworkers. They followed the marches, strikes, and boycotts intensely and many became politically motivated themselves. They joined the pickets in front of grocery stores in their own neighborhoods during the grape boycott and began to sing and chant the slogans of Chavez's campesino movement that became so familiar to Hispanics. Luis Valdez's original Teatro Campesino, founded in the fields of the Chavez protests, later became a familiar rallying group to the growing Chicano movement nationwide. Chavez became a mentor for numerous political activists, who learned organizing techniques from his work and looked to his example in forming their own organizations.

Chavez's understanding of the ways in which an oppressed minority can gain economic and political power through community participation was one of the major starting points for a growing Hispanic activism, not only in California but across the country. In his later years Chavez took a measure of pride in seeing growing numbers of Hispanics as political participants. He had become a symbol for community activists, labor movement workers, and young Hispanics as they began their own work. "Once social change begins it cannot be reversed," Chavez said, and continued,

> You cannot uneducate the person who has learned to read. You cannot humiliate the person who feels pride. You cannot oppress the people who are not afraid anymore. Our opponents must understand that it's not just the union we have built—unions like other institutions can come and go—but we're more than institutions. For nearly 20 years, our union has been on the cutting edge of a people's cause, and you cannot do away with an entire people and you cannot stamp out a people's cause. La causa, our cause, doesn't have to be experienced twice. The consciousness and pride that were raised by our union are alive and thriving inside millions of young Hispanics who will never work on a farm.[6]

Antonio Vasquez remembers his first connection with the UFW as an event that changed his life. In 1966, he was a community organizer for a church-based social organization in a Puerto Rican neighborhood in Chicago. Born in Chicago to Mexican immigrants, Vasquez was young, relatively new to the business of organizing, and lacking a clear idea of what might be ahead for himself and his organization. Vasquez's boss, an admirer of Cesar Chavez, sent him, along with two other Chicago activists, to participate in the UFW march to Sacramento.

"And that's when the metamorphosis occurred," Vasquez said later. "I couldn't relate to the civil rights struggle because it didn't get under my skin, and that particular trip all of a sudden was life—everything began to fall in. And by the time I got to Sacramento I was like completely vulnerable. And that's when I got to meet the guys who were organizing...."[7]

"I remember working in 120 degree heat," said Refugio Serrano, 87, who worked in the Central Valley grape fields alongside the union organizer for 90 cents an hour. "The ranchers, they did not care. They did not offer us water or supply toilets. Cesar called strikes. We marched. He made them give us water."[8]

Antonia Saludado was a Delano, California, teenager when she quit school to work in the fields to help support her family. She became a Cesar Chavez supporter early on. When Chavez asked some of the local workers to travel to various cities to spread the word about the union and its grape boycott, she left Delano with others for Chicago. She only spoke Spanish and, except for Mexico, where she was born, had never been anywhere except Delano. In union halls, church meeting rooms, and on picket lines, she worked with fervor and commitment. It was Chavez, she says, who gave her confidence and strength to overcome her fears. "That's something the old man taught me: not to be afraid."[9]

RETURN TO THE FIELDS

Chavez continued to campaign against pesticides into the 1990s. He continued to coordinate strikes and to speak at rallies and colleges, continually spreading the message that the battle for human rights and human safety was not yet over. He fought in the courts, as growers tried to use such legal loopholes as switching ownership rights to void previous contracts with the union. He went from town to town trying to convince consumers not to eat grapes until grapes were pesticide free.

In early 1991, he appeared before a group of organizers in Washington, D.C., brought together by consumer advocate Ralph Nader. Later that year, he worked vigorously around the state of California leading antipesticide rallies.

In December, Juana Chavez, age 99, died in San Jose. Before 300 family members, Chavez delivered a touching tribute in a church near the Chavez home in Sal Si Puedes. She, along with his father, Librado, who had died a few years earlier at the age of 100, had given Chavez a core set of beliefs in Catholicism, pacifism, pride in culture, and commitment to the poor that he had carried throughout his life and career.

In April of 1993, Chavez was in the tiny southwest Arizona town of San Luis, near Yuma, where the Chavez family, a half century earlier, had been forced out of their small farm and had begun their lives as migrant farmworkers. He was there to help UFW attorneys defend the union against a lawsuit brought by Bruce Church Inc., a giant Salinas, California–based lettuce and vegetable producer. The company sought damages of several million dollars from the union, claiming losses resulting from a union boycott of its lettuce during the 1980s. Rather than bringing the legal action in California, the company filed the suit in the conservative state of Arizona, where its attorneys believed it had a better chance of winning.

Chavez knew that winning the court battle against the Bruce Church interests was critical for the survival of the union. The financially strapped United Farm Workers was in no financial condition to absorb the kind of fine that an unfavorable verdict might inflict.

In preparing for his court appearance in the trial, Chavez began a short fast to regain moral strength. After two days on the witness stand, the union leader was exhausted but confident. He broke his fast and was taken on a drive around Yuma by long-time friend David Martinez. They toured the barrios of the south side and saw the playground where Chavez had played stickball with his brother Richard and the school where his teachers had admonished him for speaking Spanish. That evening, saying he was very tired, he took a book about Native American art with him to bed. The next morning, April 23, 1993, Martinez found his lifeless body.

On April 29, 1993, more than 40,000 mourners honored Chavez at the UFW headquarters in Delano. In caravans, the people came—entertainers, politicians, church leaders, social service directors, union leaders, and fellow associates in the UFW. But mostly the farmworkers lined up. At an all-night vigil inside a large tent, they filed past his plain pine coffin. The workers brought children of all ages. Fathers and mothers carrying infants said that they just wanted to be able to tell their children someday that they had been in the presence of a great man.

Richard built the coffin. It was something that his brother had asked him to do years before. Richard teased Chavez at the time, saying that would never be possible because Chavez would outlive him. Nevertheless, Chavez had been serious, even instructing Richard that it be a simple pine box. It took Richard nearly 40 hours to construct it; he was often interrupted by family and friends who came to watch and console him and talk about the old times.

There was a funeral march through the streets of Delano. Mourners flew the black eagle flag along with traditional black and white mourning flags. They carried white gladiolas, a Mexican mourning symbol and a favorite flower of Helen. They cried out *"Viva La Chavez!"* Marc Grossman, one of Chavez's closest spokespersons, said,

> By the superficial values many used to measure success in the 1990s, you would have to say Cesar Chavez was not very successful. He had to quit school after the eighth grade to help his family. He never owned a house. He never earned more than $6,000 a year. When he died in 1993, at age 66, he left no money for his family. Yet more than 40,000 people marched behind the plain pine casket at his funeral, honoring the more than 40 years he spent struggling to improve the lives of farm workers.[10]

Among the crowd of celebrities and long-time Chavez associates were people such as Felemon Lopez, head of a new farmworkers' union of mostly Mixtec Indians from the Mexican state of Oaxaca. Known as "Cloud People" because of the dramatic cloud formations in the sky above Oaxaca, these workers were the latest to begin the journey toward dignity and respect in the harvest fields of California. Chavez had helped pave their way.

Chavez was laid to rest at a burial site near the entrance to La Paz, just a few feet from where Boycott, his German Shepard dog, was buried. The memorial program prepared for the family bore the words that Cesar had prepared when he broke his longest fast: "It is my deepest belief that only by giving our lives do we find life," they read. "The truest act of courage, the strongest act of manliness, is to sacrifice ourselves for others in a totally non-violent struggle for justice. To be a man is to suffer for others. God help us to be men."[11]

In her eulogy, Dolores Huerta, his close partner in the UFW over the years, said that his death, at Easter time, would bind the union together once again. Her remarks echoed the religious symbolism that had characterized the movement from its beginning, from the ever-present flag of the Virgin of Guadalupe to the union's anthem, "De Colores." They sang the anthem at Chavez's burial with renewed faith that his movement would live on.

> De colores, de colores se visten los campos en la primavera . . .
> (In colors, in colors the fields dress in the spring).[12]

CARRYING THE TORCH

Unlike many of the sons and daughters of farmworkers, Cruz Gomez was able to attend a university. Her father, a farmworker outside Santa Barbara, California, had established a permanent residence and worked steadily at a regular job and was financially much better off than most of the braceros from Mexico and the seasonal migrant workers who traveled from job to job. Even in his own situation, nevertheless, Gomez's father never had a paid vacation in the 37 years that he worked the fields. As he reached middle age, his body was breaking down.

Early in her life, Gomez had heard about Chavez from her father and, now, as a college student, her sense of activism and that of some of her friends was increasingly heightened as she heard of the work of Chavez—the marches, the challenges to big business, the boycotts, and all the national attention that his work had brought to the farming communities of California. She began to follow his work with great fascination and, despite having two small children from a marriage that did not survive, she joined a student organization involved with social reform.

> For me, Chavez was it, that's all, just it. He was the main man. I remember when I met him. It was 1967 or '68, I was a college student at the University of California at Santa Barbara. I was divorced and had two small children, a kind of mother figure in the ... student organization. We went up to Delano as a group, and sat around and talked with him. It was very informal, but he was all there. He gave us his full attention.[13]

When Gomez returned to college, she changed her major from biology to sociology. Her visit to Chavez, she said, had been the difference. By 1971, she took a job working in a local community organization. She has been doing the same kind of work ever since, spending her days listening to the problems of migrant farm workers and trying in any way she can to help.

In August 1994, Chavez was posthumously awarded the Presidential Medal of Freedom, the United State's highest honor for nonmilitary personnel. Chavez's wife, Helen, accepted the award at the White House. At the ceremony, President Bill Clinton said,

> He was for his own people a Moses figure. The farm workers who labored in the fields and yearned for respect and self-sufficiency pinned their hopes on this remarkable man, who, with faith and

discipline, with soft-spoken humility and amazing inner strength, led a very courageous life. And in so doing, brought dignity to the lives of so many others, and provided for us inspiration for the rest of our nation's history.[14]

Herlinda Gonzalez stitched together her own UFW flag 40 years ago. It is now a bit faded, with the once-flaming red now somewhat pink and the black Aztec eagle turning gray. Nevertheless, she flies the flag today as she did then. She remembers the day in 1966 when the members of the farmworkers' union and their supporters marched along Highway 33 on their way to Sacramento.

The flag, and the movement it represents, she says, is "for the people who work hard and don't get paid for it, for those who don't get opportunities or education. It's for the seniors who aren't taken care of," said Gonzalez, 67, a longtime social worker who spent her summers working in the fields.[15]

Chavez had forged a movement to help those with little voice or power, "the human beings who torture their bodies, sacrifice their youth and numb their spirits to produce this great agricultural wealth, a wealth so vast that it feeds all of America and much of the world. And yet the men, women and children who are the flesh and blood of this production often do not have enough to feed themselves."[16]

He had helped them make progress. Although the numbers of workers covered by contracts with the UFW are substantially lower than in the heyday of the movement, there have been improvement in the fields. Still on the lower rung of the economic ladder, farmworkers, however, have benefits that were unheard of before the advent of the union. They are covered by workers' compensation laws. They are working for at least the minimum wage as set by the state legislature. They are living and working in conditions improved from those Chavez faced as a young man in the fields. No longer are farmworkers slaves to the short-handled hoe.

Ricardo LaForel marched for the UFW in Colorado in 1972 with thousands of workers who came from all over the state. "It took us four days. We would stop and sleep on the side of the road," he says. "I really felt like we were almost doing God's work. When we do for the poor among us, we're doing work that the Almighty would've wanted us to do." LaForel went on to work with a Colorado state agency whose mission was to help migrant workers.[17]

When Chavez Delgado, one of Cesar's many grandchildren, walks the streets of San Jose, his grandfather is never far from his mind. "This area has so many ties to my grandfather and his work," Delgado said. "This is where he began organizing. The site of the Mexican Heritage Plaza used to be a Safeway, which itself was the site of one of the first boycotts here in San Jose against lettuce and grapes." He says, "I look at these kids and think, perhaps we have the next Cesar Chavez right now, walking around here in San Jose."[18]

A reporter once asked Chavez, "What accounts for all the affection and respect so many farm workers show you in public?" Chavez looked down and smiled. He said, "The feeling is mutual."[19]

NOTES

1. Jeffrey St. Clair, "Render unto Cesar: Songs and Dances from the Fields of Pain," *Dissident Voice*, 12 April 2003, http://www.dissidentvoice.org/Articles4/StClair_Chavez.htm.

2. Ibid.

3. "Interview with Tomás A. Villanueva," http://depts.washington.edu/pcls/ufw/tomas_villanueva.htm.

4. Ibid.

5. "Lessons of Dr. Martin Luther King, Jr.," Cesar Chavez, 12 January 1990, http://www.sfsu.edu/~cecipp/cesar_chavez/cesarmlk.htm.

6. Cesar Chavez, "What the Future Holds for Farm Workers and Hispanics," Speech at the Commonwealth Club, San Francisco, 9 November 1984, http://www.mindfully.org/Reform/Cesar-Chavez9nov84.htm.

7. Geoffrey Fox, *Hispanic Nation: Culture, Politics, and the Constructing of Identity* (Tucson: University of Arizona Press, 1996), 120.

8. Angelica Pence, "Exhibition Honors Cesar Chavez / Farm Union Leader's Writings, Smithsonian Items on Display," *San Francisco Chronicle*, 4 September 2000, 13.

9. Karima A. Haynes, "Oral History Project Explores UFW Roots," *Los Angeles Times*, 11 August 2002, B4.

10. Marc Grossman, "By Giving Our Lives, We Find Life," http://www.soup4world.com/ssli/cesarchavez.html.

11. Ibid.

12. Michael Richmond, "The Music of Labor: From Movement to Culture," *Legal Studies Forum* (1999), http://tarlton.law.utexas.edu/lpop/etext/lsf/richm23.htm.

13. Frank Bardacke, "Cesar's Ghost," *The Nation* (26 July 1993), 130.

14. "Remarks by the President of the United States in Medal of Freedom Ceremony," The White House, Office of the Press Secretary, 8 August 1994, http://www.medaloffreedom.com/1994Recipients.htm.

15. Todd Milbourn, "Chavez's Path: Progress, Pain," *Modesto Bee*, 4 April 2004, http://www.modbee.com/local/story/8368479p-9189702c.html.

16. Marc Grossman, "Chavez, Steinbeck: The Ties That Bind," http://www.findarticles.com/p/articles/mi_m0MKY/is_9_27/ai_108881867.

17. Cindy Rodriguez, "Cesar Chavez Led the Way to Peaceful Change," *Denver Post*, 26 March 2004, B1.

18. Maria Alicia Gaura, "Celebrated with Holiday," *San Francisco Chronicle*, 30 March 2001, 3.

19. Marc Grossman, "By Giving Our Lives."

SELECTED BIBLIOGRAPHY

BOOKS

Ballis, George. *Basta! The Tale of Our Struggle*. Delano, CA: Farm Workers Press, 1966.

De Ruiz, Dana Catherine, and Richard Larios. *La Causa: The Migrant Farmworker Story*. Austin: Raintree Steck-Vaughn, 1993.

Dunne, John Gregory. *Delano: The Story of the California Grape Strike*. New York: Farrar, Straus and Giroux, 1967.

Ferriss, Susan, and Ricardo Sandoval. *The Fight in the Fields: Cesar Chavez and the Farmworkers Movement*. New York: Paradigm Productions, Inc., 1997.

Fox, Geoffrey. *Hispanic Nation: Culture, Politics, and the Constructing of Identity*. Tucson: University of Arizona Press, 1996.

Fusco, Paul, and George D. Horowitz. *La Causa: The California Grape Strike*. New York: Collier, 1970.

Galarza, Ernesto. *Spiders in the House and Workers in the Field*. Notre Dame: University of Indiana Press, 1970.

Griswold del Castillo, Richard, and Richard A. Garcia. *Cesar Chavez: A Triumph of Spirit*. Norman: University of Oklahoma Press, 1995.

Hammerback, C. John, J. Richard Jensen, and Angel Jose Gutierrez. *A War of Words: Chicano Protest in the 1960s and 1970s*. Westport, CT: Greenwood Press, 1985.

Jenkins, J. Craig. *The Politics of Insurgency: The Farm Worker Movement in the 1960s*. New York: Columbia University Press, 1985.

Levy, Jacques E. *Cesar Chavez: Autobiography of La Causa*. New York: W. W. Norton & Company, 1975.

Light, Ken, Roger Minick, and Reesa Tansey. *In These Fields*. Oakland: Harvest Press, 1982.

London, Joan, and Henry Anderson. *So Shall Ye Reap: The Story of Cesar Chavez and the Farm Workers' Movement*. New York: Thomas Crowell Company, 1970.

Matthiessen, Peter. *Sal Si Puedes: Cesar Chavez and the New American Revolution*. New York: Dell Publishing Company, 1969.

Meister, Dick, and Anne Loftis. *A Long Time Coming: The Struggle to Unionize America's Farm Workers*. New York: Macmillan, 1977.

Ross, Fred. *Conquering Goliath: Cesar Chavez at the Beginning*. Keene, CA: El Taller Grafico Press/United Farm Workers, 1989.

Taylor, Ronald. *Chavez and the Farm Workers*. Boston: Beacon Press, 1975.

Wells, Miriam. *Strawberry Fields: Politics, Class and Work in California Agriculture*. Ithaca, NY: Cornell University Press, 1996.

Zeta, Oscar Acosta. *The Revolt of the Cockroach People*. New York: Vintage Books, 1989.

PERIODICALS

Bardacke, Frank. "Cesar's Ghost." *The Nation* (26 July 1993), 130–134.

Buckley, William F. "Don't Eat Grapes Along With Me." *National Review* (15 July 1969), 60.

Chavez, Cesar. "The Organizer's Tale." *Ramparts* 5, no. 2 (1966), 43–50.

"Chavez: One Battle Ends, Another Begins." *U.S. News & World Report* (10 August 1970), 49–51.

"Cesar's Triumph." *Newsweek* (21 March 1977), 70.

"Cesar's War," *Time* (22 March 1968), 23.

Degnan, J. P. "Monopoly in the Vineyards: Grapes of Wrath Strike." *Nation* (7 February 1966), 151–154.

Griffith, Winthrop. "Is Chavez Beaten?," *New York Times Magazine* (15 September 1974), 18–20.

"Letter from Delano." *Christian Century* (23 April 1969), 539–540.

Meister, Dick. "'La Huelga' Becomes 'La Causa'," *New York Times Magazine* (17 November 1968), 63–92.

"Nonviolence Still Works." *Look* (1 April 1969), 52–55.

"Rendering unto Cesar." *Time* (22 September 1975), 32.

Seagraves, Vernal. "Cesar Chavez and the Farm Workers: Victories, Yes, but the Struggle Goes On." *The Christian Century* (17 December 1975), 1161.

"Seething Vineyards." *Newsweek* (8 July 1968), 62.

Taylor, Ronald. "Huelga! The Boycott That Worked." *Nation* (7 September 1970), 167–169.

"Tilting with the System." *Christian Century* (18 February 1970), 204–207.

Michael Yates, "A Union Is Not a 'Movement,'" *The Nation* (19 November 1977), 518.

INTERNET

California Curriculum Project Hispanic Biographies, http://www.sfsu.edu/~cecipp/cesar_chavez/chavezhome.htm.

Chavez, Cesar: "The Mexican-American and the Church," 8–10 March 1968, http://www.americanrhetoric.com/speeches/chavezspeech.htm.

_____. "Lessons of Dr. Martin Luther King, Jr.," 12 January 1990, http://www.sfsu.edu/~cecipp/cesar_chavez/cesarmlk.htm.

_____. "What the Future Holds for Farm Workers and Hispanics," Speech at the Commonwealth Club, San Francisco, http://www.mindfully.org/Reform/Cesar-Chavez9nov84.htm.

Clarren, Rebecca. "Harvesting Poison," 29 September 2003, http://www.headwatersnews.org/HCN.farmworkers.html.

Cohn, Marjorie. "The Death of El Cortito," http://www.truthout.org/docs_2005/L012505A.shtml.

Grace, Ellen. "*La Causa para La Rasa*: The Educative Processes and Development of Knowledge in the United Farm Workers From 1962 to 1970," http://scholar.lib.vt.edu/theses/available/etd-3198-194743.

Grossman, Marc. "By Giving Our Lives, We Find Life," http://www.soup4world.com/ssli/cesarchavez.html

Furumoto, Kim Benita. "Viva La Causa! Cesar Chavez Remembered." *Diatribe*, May 1993, http://www.sfsu.edu/~cecipp/cesar_chavez/remembered.htm.

"Interview with Guadalupe Gamboa, 9 April 2003," http://depts.washington.edu/pcls/ufw/guadalupe_gamboa.htm.

"Interview with Tomás A. Villanueva," "http://depts.washington.edu/pcls/ufw/Tomas%20.Villanueva.pdf.

Irrgang, Ken. "Cesar Chavez: A Spiritual Man," http://www.the-tidings.com/2004/0402/cesar.htm.

Jones, Carol. "Dolores Huerta: Cesar Chavez' Partner in Founding the United Farm Workers Union in California," http://www.csupomona.edu/~jis/1997/Mullikin.pdf.

Levy, Jacques. *Cesar Chavez: Autobiography of La Causa*, http://chavez.cde.ca.gov/ModelCurriculum/Teachers/Lessons/Resources/Documents/Chavez_Biography_by_Levy.PDF.

Martin, Douglas. "Jim Drake, 63, an Organizer of Workers and a 60's Boycott, Dies," 9 September 2001, http://lists.village.virginia.edu/lists_archive/sixties-l/3507.html.

Quintanilla, Antita. "Remembering a Modest Cesar," http://www.azteca.net/aztec/modest_cesar.html.

"A Rare, Unheralded Champion of American Workers, 22 February 2004, http://www.epinions.com/content_3786842244.

St. Clair, Jeffrey. "Render unto Cesar: Songs and Dances from the Fields of Pain," *Dissident Voice*, 12 April 2003, http://www.dissidentvoice.org/Articles4/StClair_Chavez.htm.

Schwartz, Ed. "Cesar Chavez: Leader as Organizer." http://www.iscv.org/Opportunity/CesarChavez/cesarchavez.html.

"Viva la Causa: Cesar E. Chavez, Interviewed by Wendy Goepel," originally published in *Farm Labor* 1, no. 5 (April 1964), available at http://www.sfsu.edu/~cecipp/cesar_chavez/lacausa.htm.

MANUSCRIPTS

Microfilm FBI File on Cesar Chavez and United Farm Workers. Wilmington, Delaware: Scholarly Resources, 1995, 2 reels.

Papers of Cesar Chavez, Walter P. Reuther Library, Wayne State University, Detroit, Michigan.

INDEX

About the Author

ROGER BRUNS is a prolific writer and biographer with titles such as *Preacher: Billy Sunday and Big-Time American Evangelism* (1992), *Billy Graham: A Biography* (Greenwood, 2004), and *Jesse Jackson: A Biography* (Greenwood, 2005).